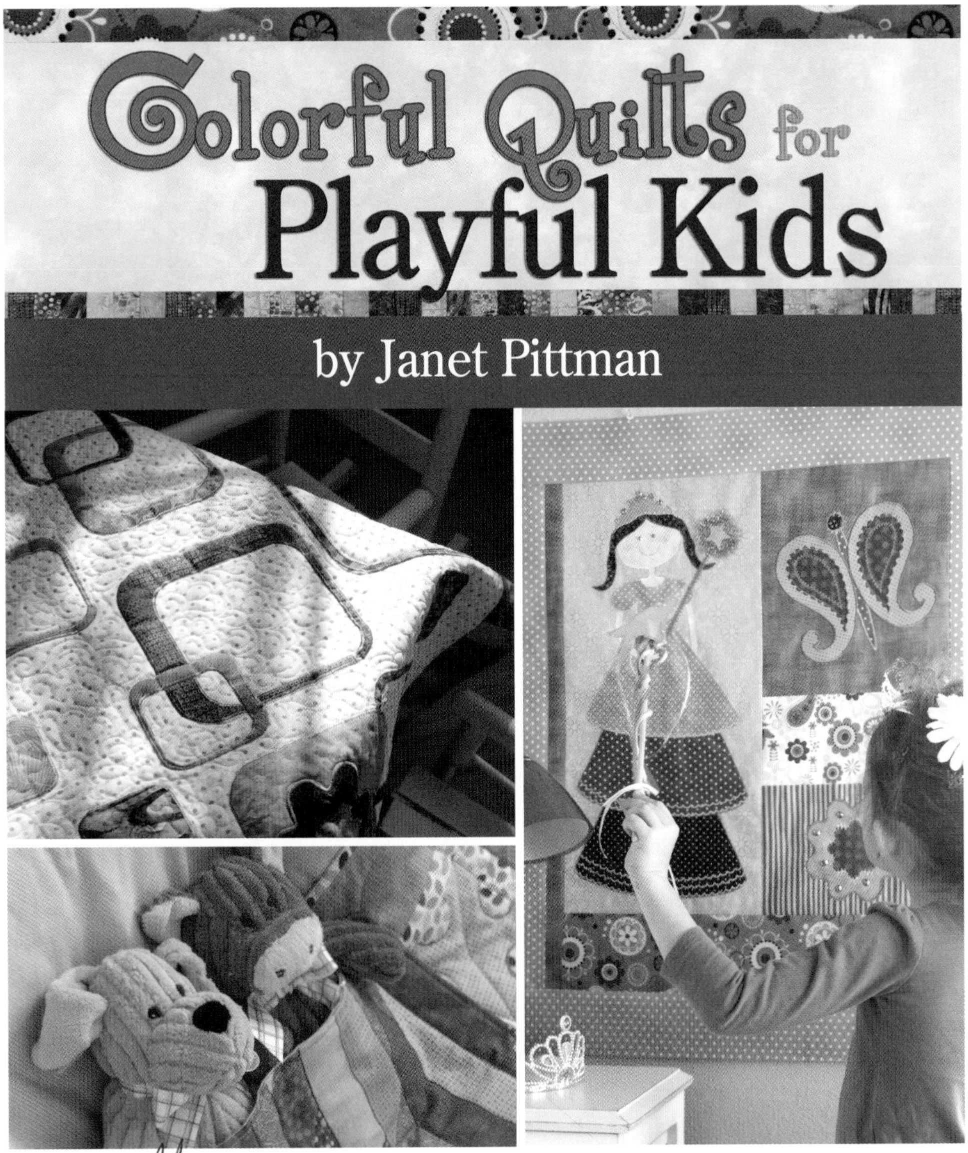

Colorful Quilts for Playful Kids

by Janet Pittman

Landauer Publishing, LLC

This book was designed, produced, and
published by Landauer Publishing, LLC
3100 101st Street, Urbandale, IA 50322
800-557-2144; 515-287-2144; www.landauerpub.com

President/Publisher: Jeramy Lanigan Landauer
Vice President of Sales and Administration: Kitty Jacobson
Editor: Jeri Simon
Art Director: Laurel Albright
Creative Director: Janet Pittman
Photographer: Sue Voegtlin
Contributing Photographer: Lyne Neymeyer

This book is printed on acid-free paper.

Printed in United States 10 9 8 7 6 5 4 3 2 1

Library of Congress Control Number: 2012937349

ISBN 13: 978-1-935726-25-8

Acknowledgements

Special thanks to the following people:

Kris Peterson

for her technical expertise and never-ending encouragement through all phases of this book.

Nan Earll

who spent several days of precise piecing and stitching appliqué.

Kelly Van Vliet

of Quilts by Kelly for her expert quilting on several of the quilts in this book.

Lyne Neymeyer

who listens as I bounce design ideas around and helps me refine them.

All of the quilting grandmothers

who shared tips for getting their grandchildren involved in the quilting process.

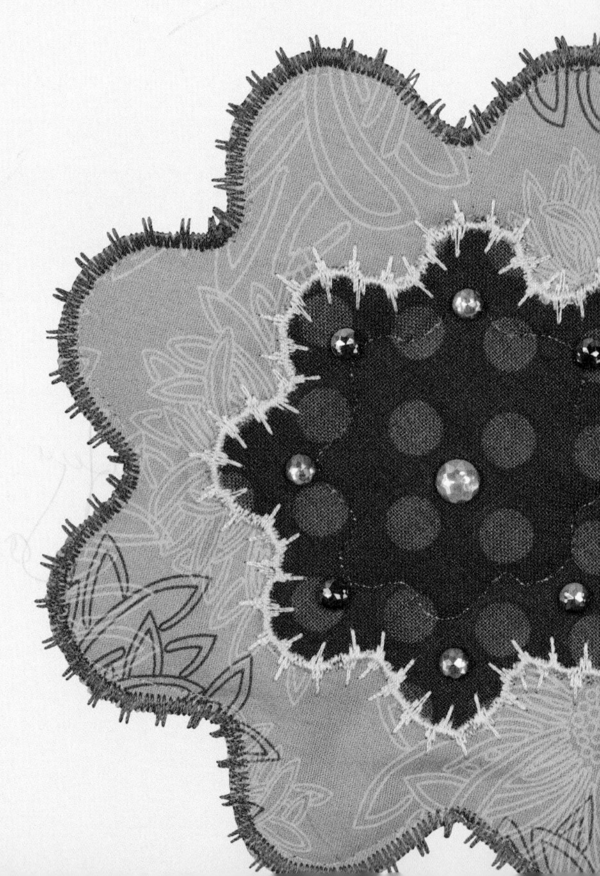

Table of Contents

Introduction

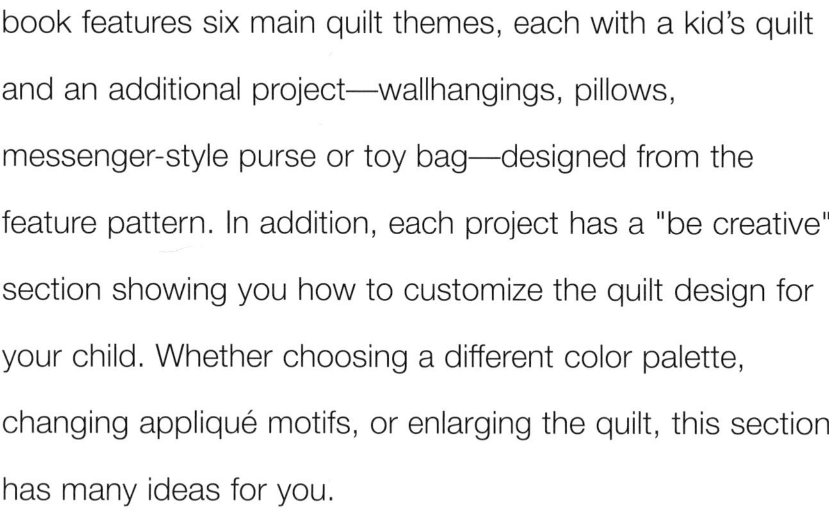

Colorful Quilts for Playful Kids

All quilters, whether moms or grandmas, want to make a special quilt for the kids in their lives. This book features six main quilt themes, each with a kid's quilt and an additional project—wallhangings, pillows, messenger-style purse or toy bag—designed from the feature pattern. In addition, each project has a "be creative" section showing you how to customize the quilt design for your child. Whether choosing a different color palette, changing appliqué motifs, or enlarging the quilt, this section has many ideas for you.

On the next few pages are ideas for getting the kids in your life involved in the quilt design and creative process. I know they are already playing with your fabric, tape measures, and threads.

I have designed many kids' quilt patterns under my label Garden Trellis Designs, but my two granddaughters inspired me to look at this design style with fresh ideas. I hope you'll enjoy making colorful quilts for the kids in your life.

Janet

Contact Janet at jan@gardentrellisdesigns.com or visit her website, www.gardentrellisdesigns.com.

Getting Kids Involved—Helping Kids Enjoy Your Hobby

We all hope our kids and grandkids will love quilting as much as we do. Following are a few suggestions for fun activities to get the kids involved. Some are general ideas for doing things with kids in your sewing room and others are specific to a quilt in this book. The most important thing is that the kids are having fun alongside you.

In the Sewing Room

- Give kids a magnet to scour the room for those pins that seem to multiply on the floor.
- Let kids help you arrange blocks on your design wall or the floor.
- Give your children a light-colored square of fabric and a smooth surface to draw on. In the example, fabric crayons are used to color a rainbow and fabric markers are used to color in a beach ball. Or, let them make their own design. Heat set the fabric crayons or markers according to manufacturer's directions. They can also rub the crayons over purchased or found textures. For more ideas see peek-a-boo blocks on page 13.

tips

- For a smoother stiffer surface, back the fabric with freezer paper.
- A poly/cotton blend fabric will give brighter colors with fabric crayons than 100 percent cotton.

- Talk with younger children about the rainbow and have them select colors from your stash. They can also choose warm and cool colors. For older kids, have them work with the color wheel and the variety of color hues, shades, tones, tints, and color schemes. This idea also works with thread.

- For a kids coloring activity before you start a project or to keep someone busy while you are stitching, give them paper copies of the appliqué motifs. After they are colored, cut out, overlap, and glue together with paper glue.
- Let the kids make fabric collages with fabric from your scrap box. Give them glue and construction paper or fabric backed with freezer paper. In addition to fabric and yarn, include wrapping or decorative papers and scissors appropriate to your child's age. For little ones who want to cut scraps, there are some blunt-tipped scissors available that will cut fabric.

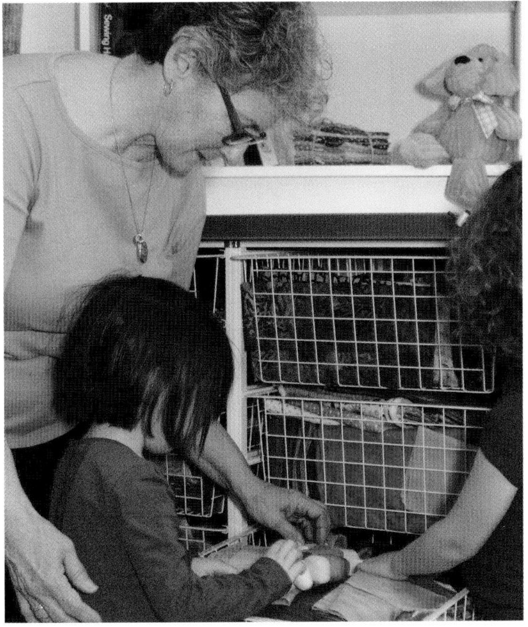

Picking fabric from Grandma's stash.

Getting Kids Involved—More Ideas

Additional activities for featured quilt projects.

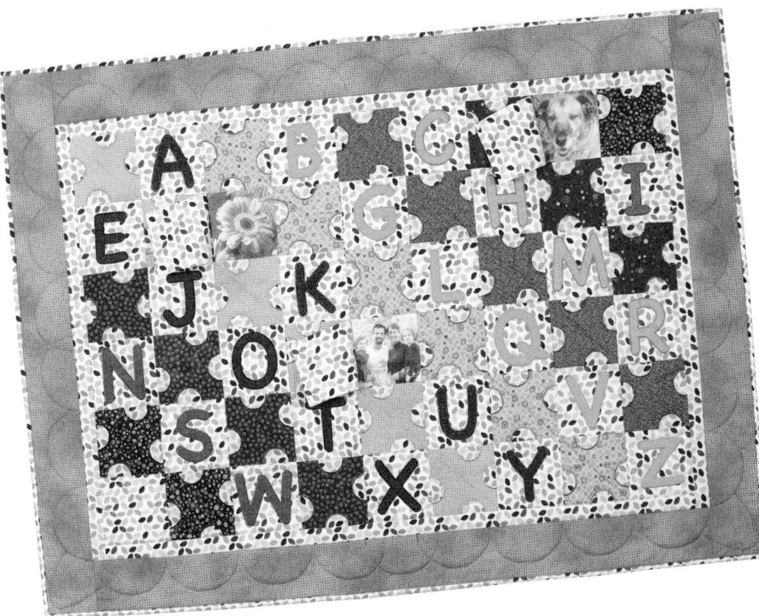

- For the Alphabet Puzzle quilt, let your helpers choose several photos, I Spy fabrics, or make small drawings to place behind letters of the alphabet for personalized alphabet blocks. Refer to page 13.

- Have kids select a design from the smaller appliqué motifs and fuse to an apron. Refer to Preparing Appliqué on page 110. You can also reduce one of the larger motifs. Stitch around the design or use heavy-weight fusible web. You can find plain child-sized aprons at craft stores.

- When choosing colors for their own quilt, start with a print, even if it won't be used in the quilt. Have the youngster help select fabric in colors from the print. For example, the Paisley Princess quilt, above, and on page 40 started with the border fabric and a granddaughter who loves purple. Alphabet Puzzle, at left, started with the multicolored jelly bean fabric. Some additional fabric samples that can be used as color inspiration are shown.

You are the best judge

Younger children like to start at the sewing machine in an adult's lap with their hands under the adult's guiding the fabric. An older child can stand at the machine to use the foot pedal or put the foot pedal on a box and work by themselves. The same rules apply to using an iron. You are the best judge of each child's abilities. Always supervise and teach kids to ask for permission before using potentially dangerous tools and appliances.

Getting Kids Involved—Block Play

Introduce your kids to patchwork with these easy, fun ideas.

- For patchwork blocks to color, use Block Play Grids on page 128, or draft your own by drawing a 7" square and dividing it horizontally and vertically into three 2½" sections. Add diagonal lines to make desired blocks. Set out crayons, pencils, or markers and let the kids design their own blocks.
- For Block Play Puzzles, add color and real fabric texture by making fabric puzzle pieces. For the game boards copy the Block Play Grids on page 128 at 300%.
- For examples of traditional block light/dark color combinations, copy the colored blocks on page 127.

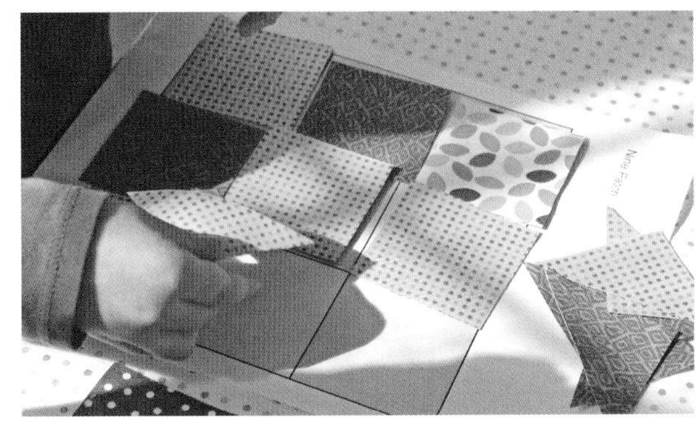

Block Play Puzzles

1. For 7½" block puzzles, make two-sided puzzle pieces by fusing contrasting fabrics together. Refer to Preparing Appliqué on page 110.
2. For each set, cut 2–8" squares of paper-backed fusible web and 2–8" squares of contrasting fabrics. Make two sets of the same fabric combination.

Note: Use heavy-weight fusible web for added stiffness.

3. Fuse contrasting fabric squares together with fusible web in between.
4. Trim each fused square to 7½". Cut squares into three 2½"-wide rectangles and then cut the rectangles into 9–2½" squares for a total of 18 squares.

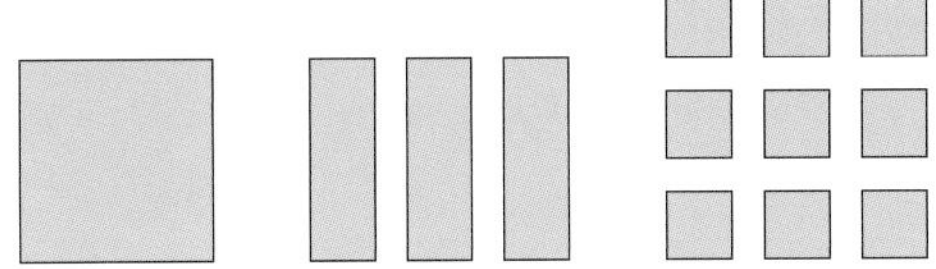

5. Cut two of the 2½" squares in half to make four rectangles.

6. Cut six of the 2½" squares in half diagonally to make half-square triangles.

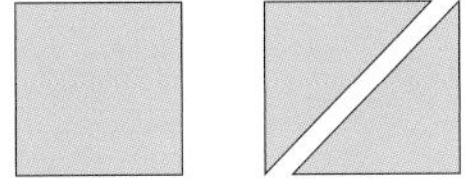

7. You should have 10–2½" squares remaining.
8. For Ohio Star and Card Trick blocks cut five of the 2½" half-square triangles in half to make quarter-square triangles.

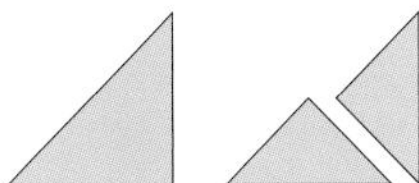

9. Make two sets of three different color combinations for extra variety.

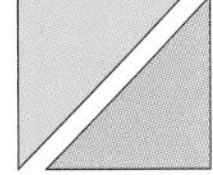 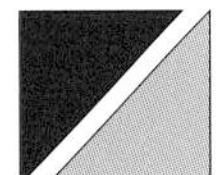 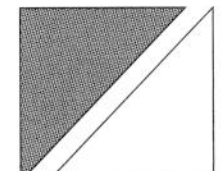

projects

This section includes six unique and colorful quilts for the kids in your life. Each project is followed by a fun adaptation of the design which varies from smaller quilts and wallhangings to pillows and bags. A "be creative" section will give you additional ideas for using these designs.

Alphabet Puzzle

finished size: 49½" x 36"

This fun alphabet quilt can be personalized for any child. For my granddaughters, I hid photos beneath D (dog), F (flower), and P (Pittman).

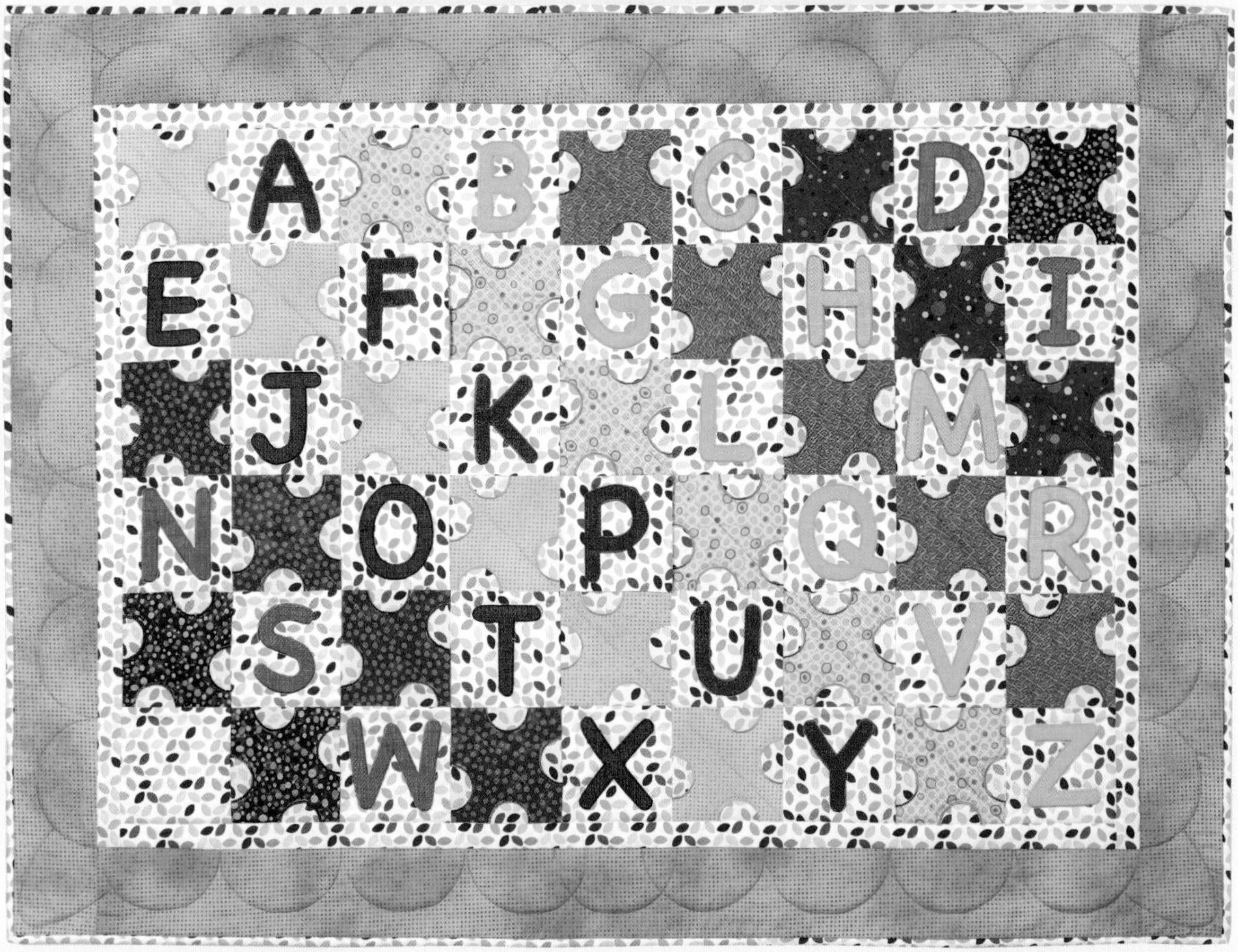

MATERIALS

Alphabet Blocks and Inner Border
- 1¼ yards white print for blocks, inner border, and binding

Puzzle Blocks
- 6 fat quarters in assorted prints in green, turquoise, orange, blue, violet, and red for puzzle blocks

Outer Border
- ¾ yard turquoise print for outer border

Appliqué
- 6 fat quarters in assorted tone-on-tone prints in red, green, turquoise, orange, blue, and violet for alphabet appliqué

Backing
- 1½ yards backing fabric

Paper-Backed Fusible Web
- 1½ yards

Hook and Loop (Velcro®) Closures
- 1 set small circles for every two peek-a-boo blocks (optional)

Quilt Batting
- 56" x 42" piece of quilt batting (or Crib-size batting)

Photo Transfer Fabric
- enough to print a 5" square for each photo desired

Fabric suggestions are 40"-42" wide. Fat quarter = 18" x 20".

Sew all patchwork seams with a ¼" seam allowance.

Follow manufacturer's directions for using paper-backed fusible web.

Cut the Quilt Pieces

From the white print cut
- 27–5" background squares for alphabet blocks
- 2–1½" x 41" top and bottom inner borders
- 2–1½" x 29½" side inner borders
- 5–2¼" strips for binding

From the green print fat quarter cut
- 6–5" squares for puzzle blocks

From the turquoise print fat quarter cut
- 6–5" squares for puzzle blocks

From the orange print fat quarter cut
- 5–5" squares for puzzle blocks

From the blue print fat quarter cut
- 3–5" squares for puzzle blocks

From the violet print fat quarter cut
- 3–5" squares for puzzle blocks

From the red print fat quarter cut
- 4–5" squares for puzzle blocks

From the turquoise print cut
- 3–4"-wide strips. Join strips, then cut 2–4" x 43" top and bottom outer borders.
- 2–4" x 36½" side outer borders

Prepare the Appliqué Pieces

Following the instructions in Preparing Fused Appliqué on page 110, make the letters and puzzle tabs. The patterns are found on pages 68-71 ("M" and "W" are the same pattern).

Alphabet Letters
- 1 of each in the colors indicated

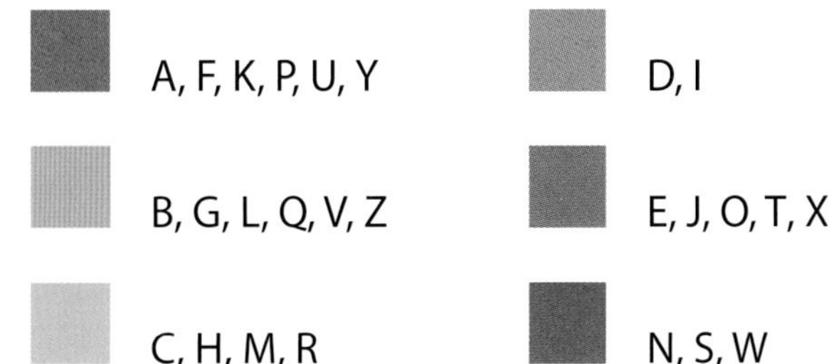

Puzzle Tabs
- 108 from white print

Stitch the Appliqué

1. Center 1 alphabet letter on each background square. Fuse in place.
2. Stitch the appliqué with a satin zigzag stitch, page 118, using thread matching the alphabet letter.
3. Position 4 puzzle tabs on each puzzle block square, aligning straight edge of puzzle tab with edge of background square. Place the tabs slightly off center on each side, no closer than 1¹⁄₄" from corner. Fuse in place.

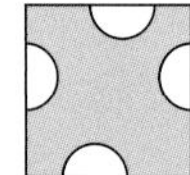 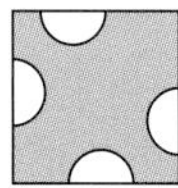 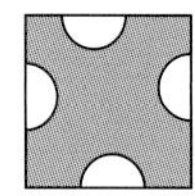 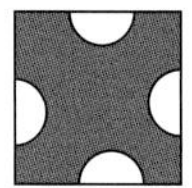

Note: Work on a non-stick pressing sheet to protect your pressing surface.

4. Stitch the curved edge of puzzle tabs with a satin zigzag stitch using thread matching the puzzle block square.

Make Personalized Alphabet Blocks

If personalizing the blocks follow these directions for each personalized alphabet block. See "be creative" on page 13 for more ideas for peek-a-boo block options.

1. Following Transferring Photos to Fabric instructions on page 125, and manufacturer's instructions, prepare image and print on prepared fabric. Trim prepared image to 5" square.
2. Cut 1 white print 5" square for flap facing.
3. Place 1 appliquéd alphabet block and 5" facing square with right sides together. Stitch top, right side, and bottom of flap starting and ending with a slightly wider seam allowance.

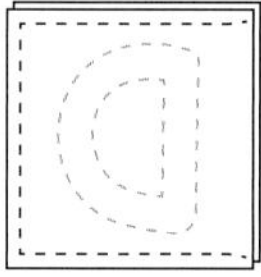

4. Trim corners and turn flap right side out; press.
5. Baste flap to prepared image along unstitched left edge.

6. Treat each personalized alphabet block as a unit when joining blocks and rows, taking care not to catch turned edges of flap in seam allowances.

Assemble the Quilt

1. Arrange the alphabet blocks, puzzle blocks, and remaining white print square.
2. Join into rows; join rows to complete quilt center.

3. Sew the white print inner top and bottom borders to the quilt center. Sew the white print inner side borders to the quilt center.
4. Repeat with the turquoise print outer borders.

Finish the Quilt

1. Layer the quilt top, batting, and backing.
2. Refer to Quilting Appliqué on page 126 and quilt as desired.
3. Trim the excess batting and backing to straighten the edges and square the corners.
4. Stitch together the white print 2¹⁄₄"-wide strips with diagonal seams to make a continuous strip. Use to bind the quilt.
5. If desired, add hook and loop (Velcro®) closures to flaps and image after quilt is finished. Cut hook and loop circles into quarters to fit in the two corners.

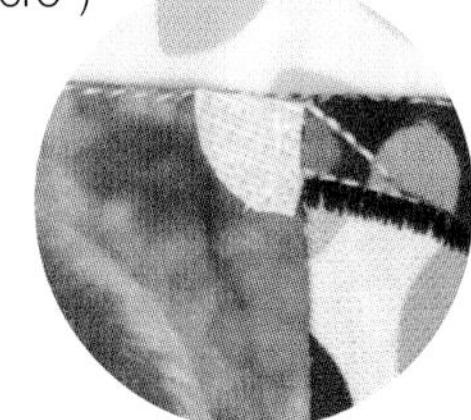

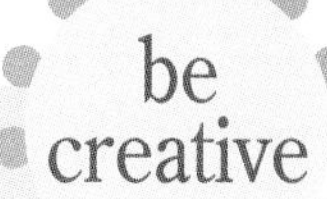

Alphabet Puzzle

Peek-A-Boo Blocks

Once you determine how many photos or images you want under the letters, there are several ways to get kids involved.

- Choose some photos from the family album then let the kids decide which ones to use. For the Alphabet Puzzle my granddaughters and I chose my dog for the "D", a close-up of a gerbera daisy flower for the "F", and the kids' family for the "P". Review Transferring Photos to Fabric on page 125 for more information.

- Have the kids draw and color pictures on fabric. See page 5 to set up for coloring on fabric. Use fabric crayons or markers and follow manufacturer's setting instructions. You can draw or trace the object onto the fabric and have the children color it. You can also use motifs from various sections of this book for outlines. Remember to reduce the size to fit the 4½" finished format.

- Have the kids help choose I Spy fabrics to go under a few of the letters.
- Take a piece of your child's artwork, scan it and print to fabric. Refer to page 125.
- To give the alphabet flaps a more decorative look, sew on 12" lengths of ribbon as ties instead of the hook and loop closures. You can also use snaps.

Sports Wallhanging

finished size 20½" x 34"

Looking for a wallhanging for the ballplayer in your family? Use any combination of the nine ball patterns and layouts found on pages 74-75.

- Choose a colorful stripe or a sports-themed print for the border fabric and a coordinating light fabric for the puzzle backgrounds and tabs. Use a coordinating medium fabric for the tabbed blocks.
- To construct this wallhanging use the basic sewing directions for Springtime for Baby on page 14. Cut the inner and outer borders to the measurements shown on the illustration.
- Make two blocks with four tabs, five blocks with three tabs and two blocks with two tabs on adjoining sides.
- For the balls, be realistic or fanciful or choose to make some in the colors of a favorite sports team.

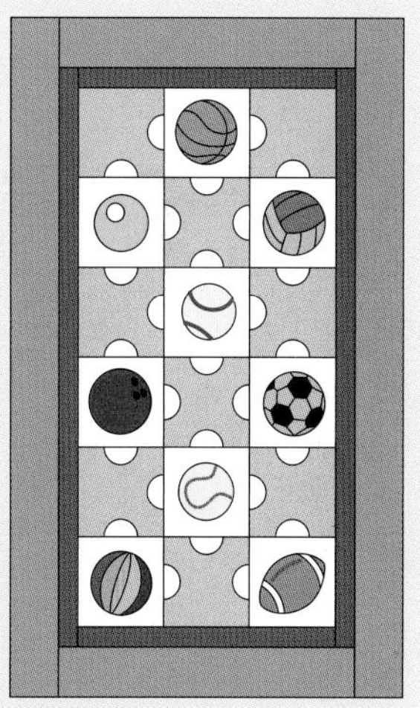

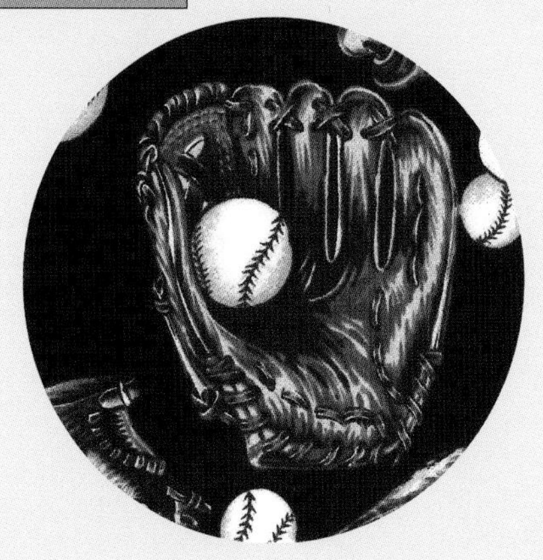

Springtime for Baby

finished size: 36" x 36"

Turn Alphabet Puzzle into a flannel quilt in bright pastels as a cozy welcome for a new arrival.

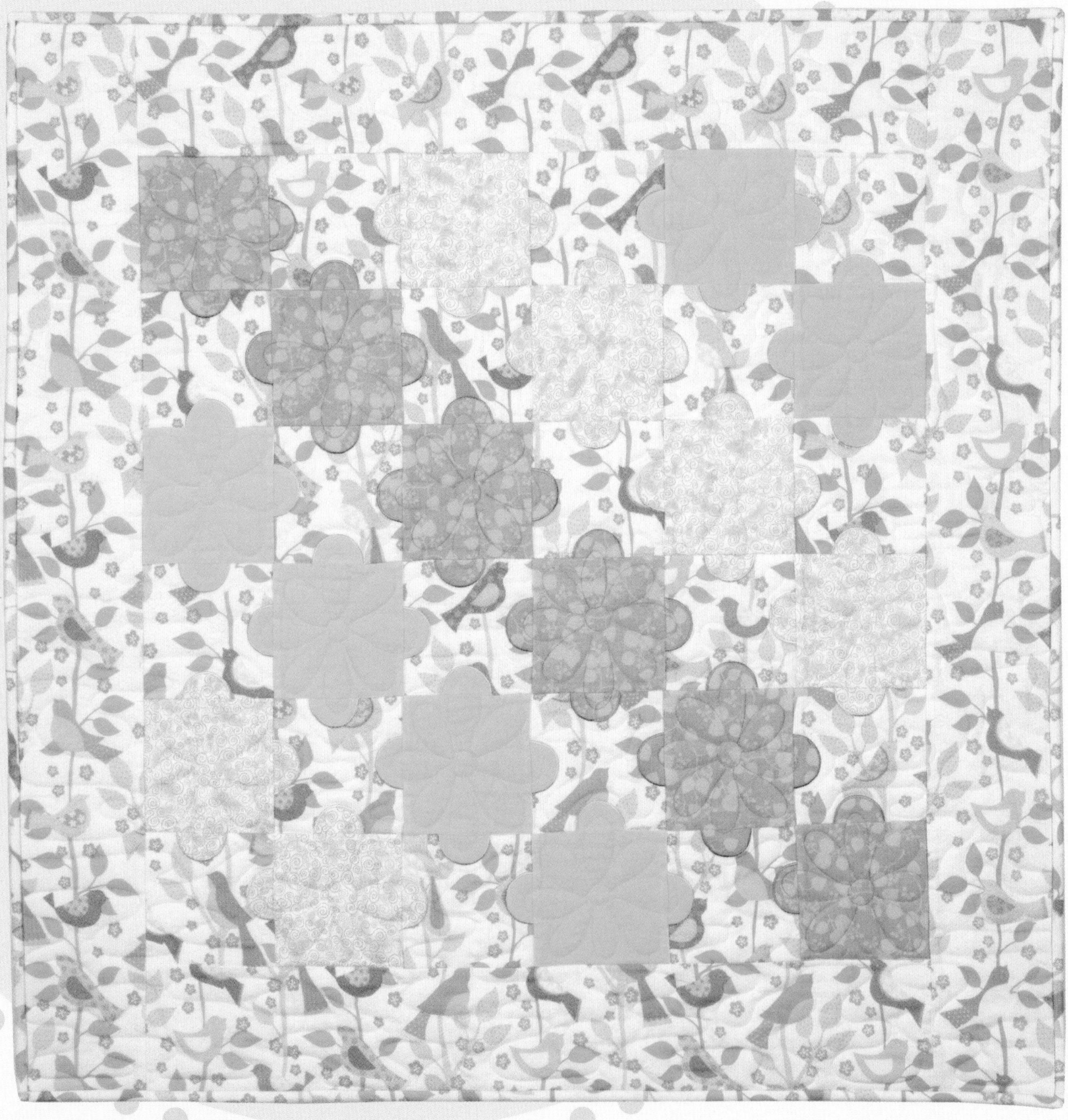

MATERIALS

Blocks, Border, and Binding

- 1½ yards yellow print flannel for blocks, border, and binding

Puzzle Blocks

- A total of 3 fat quarters in turquoise, green, and yellow tone-on-tone flannel prints for puzzle blocks

Paper-Backed Fusible Web

- ½ yard

Backing

- 1¼ yards flannel backing fabric

Quilt Batting

- 42" x 42" piece of quilt batting (or Crib-size batting)

Fabric suggestions are 40"-42" wide. Fat quarter = 18" x 20".

Sew all patchwork seams with a ¼" seam allowance.

Follow manufacturer's directions for using paper-backed fusible web.

Cut the Quilt Pieces

From the yellow print cut

- 4–2½" strips for binding
- 2–5" x 36½" side borders, see tip below
- 2–5" x 27½" top and bottom borders
- 18–5" squares

From each tone-on-tone fat quarter cut

- 6–5" squares

For Directional Fabric

If fabric is directional, cut 2–5"-wide LENGTHWISE strips after cutting the binding strips. Then cut remaining fabric into 5"-wide crosswise strips.

Prepare the Appliqué Pieces

Following the instructions in Preparing Fused Appliqué on page 110, make the following appliqué pieces. The puzzle tab pattern is found on page 68.

- 20 turquoise–Puzzle Tab
- 20 yellow–Puzzle Tab
- 20 green–Puzzle Tab

Stitch the Appliqué

1. Referring to the chart below, Position puzzle tabs on yellow print squares, aligning straight edge of puzzle tab with edge of yellow square. The puzzle tabs are centered on sides of yellow print squares. Fuse in place.

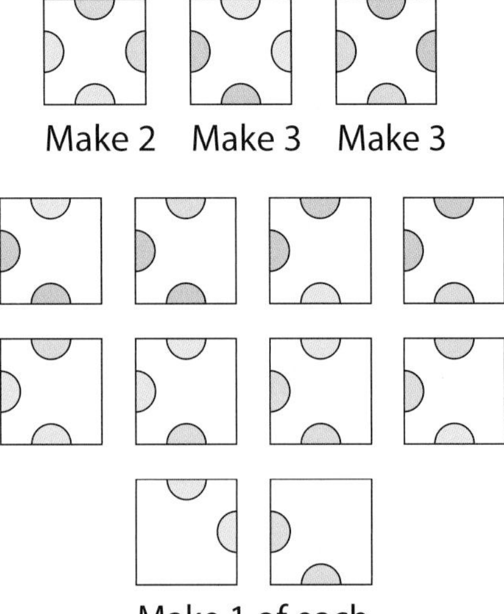

Note: Work on a non-stick pressing sheet to protect your pressing surface.

2. Stitch the curved edge of puzzle tabs with a satin zigzag stitch, page 118, using thread matching the tab.

Assemble the Quilt

1. Arrange the blocks and turquoise, yellow, and green squares as shown.
2. Join into rows; join rows to complete quilt center.
3. Sew the yellow print top and bottom borders to the quilt center. Sew the yellow print side borders to the quilt.

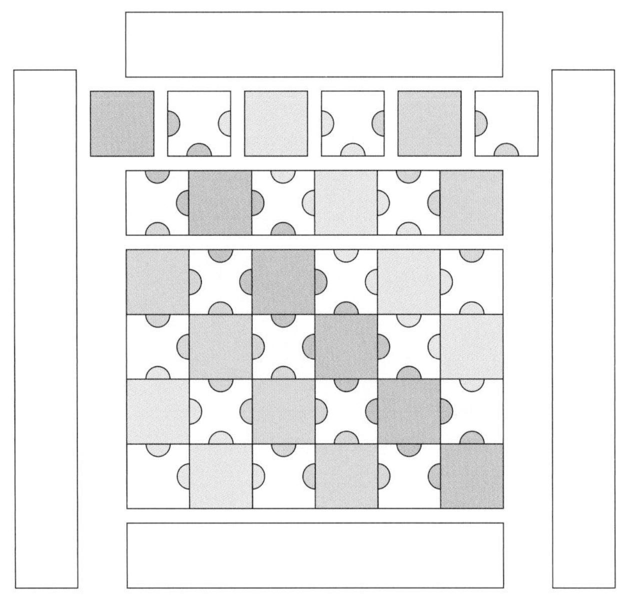

Finish the Quilt

1. Layer the quilt top, batting, and backing.
2. Refer to Quilting Appliqué on page 126 and quilt as desired.
3. Trim the excess batting and backing to straighten the edges and square the corners.
4. Stitch together the yellow print $2\frac{1}{2}$"-wide strips with diagonal seams to make a continuous strip. Use to bind the quilt.

Strippy Quilt

finished size 14" x 18"

Use leftover fabric to make a coverlet for your child's favorite companion. You can make this quilt any size—from a tiny coverlet for a little baby doll to a "giant" coverlet for a dinosaur.

MATERIALS

Quilt Top Fabric

- 2"-wide strips
- The number of strips depends on how long your scraps are and the dimensions of the quilt you want to make. For a quilt made with leftover strips from the Alphabet Puzzle fat quarters, you will need about 14-2" strips to make a small coverlet.

Backing

- 1 fat quarter

Quilt Batting

- 18" x 20" piece of quilt batting

Fabric suggestions are 2"-wide strips cut from fat quarters.

Fat quarter = 18" x 20".

Sew all patchwork seams with a ¼" seam allowance.

Cut the Quilt Pieces

From 2" strips, cut

- random pieces 5"-10" long

Assemble the Quilt

1. Join strips with diagonal seams to make 1 long strip (as for binding).

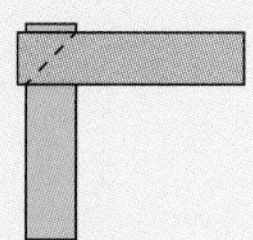

2. Cut strip into 15" sections.
3. Sew the sections together.

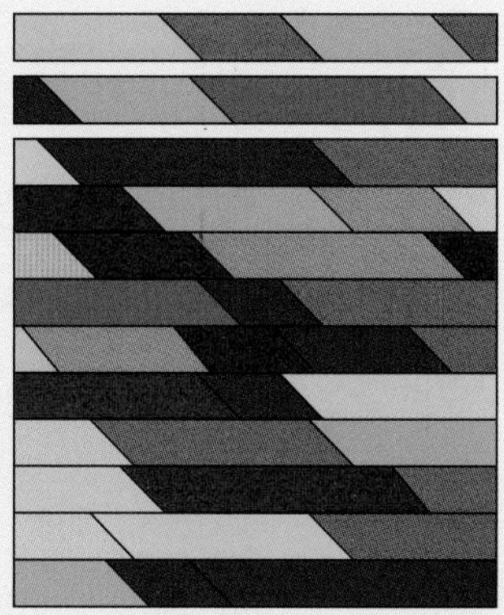

Finish the Quilt

1. Layer quilt batting, backing fabric (right side up), and quilt top (wrong side up).
2. Sew around all four sides with ¼" seam allowance, rounding corners if desired. Leave a 4" opening on one side for turning.

Tip: Mark corner curves using a large spool of thread.

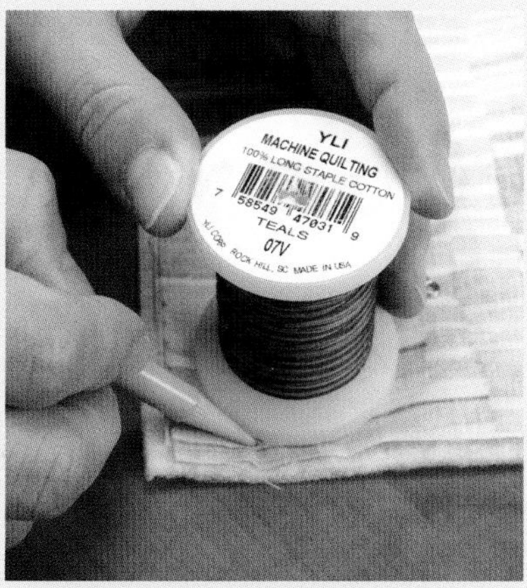

3. Trim backing and batting even with edges of quilt top. Clip or trim corners.
4. Turn right side out. Lightly press the outside edge and corners. Hand stitch the opening closed.
5. Topstitch around the top, ¼" in from the edge. Quilt in the ditch or as desired.

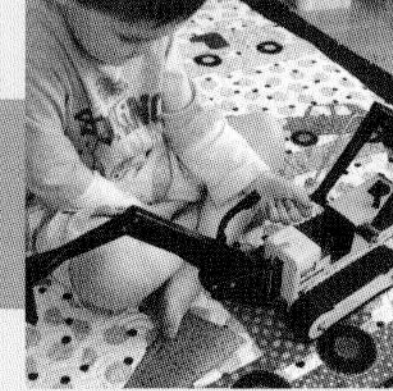

Construction Zone

finished size: 47" x 60"

Kids of all ages are fascinated by powerful construction vehicles. This colorful quilt has them all!

MATERIALS

Background
- 1⅝ yards white print

Outer Border
- 1¼ yards black print

Ground and Binding
- ¾ yard multicolor print

Inner Border and Construction Zone Letters
- ½ yard yellow tone-on-tone print

Appliqué
- 3 fat quarters in blue prints (light, medium and dark) for "roads"
- Fat quarters or smaller assorted prints in blue, turquoise, green, orange, gold, yellow, red, and purple for vehicles and dirt and gray and black for wheels

Backing
- 3 yards backing fabric

Paper-Backed Fusible Web
- 3½ yards

Quilt Batting
- 53" x 66" piece of quilt batting (or Twin-size batting)

Fabric suggestions are 40"-42" wide.

Fat quarter = 18" x 20".

If your fabric does not have 41½" of useable width, you may need to piece some pieces.

Sew all patchwork seams with a ¼" seam allowance.

Follow manufacturer's directions for using paper-backed fusible web.

Cut the Quilt Pieces

From the white print cut

- 1–12½" x 40" rectangle for Row A background
- 1–17½" x 40" rectangle for Row B background
- 1–12½" x 41½" rectangle for Row C background
  Note: If necessary, cut 2–12½"-wide strips. Join strips, then cut 1–12½" x 41½" Row C background.

From the black print cut

- 3–7½"-wide strips. Join strips, then cut 2–7½" x 43" top and bottom outer borders.
  Note: Borders will be trimmed to correct length after letters are appliquéd.
- 3–3½"-wide strips. Join strips, then cut 2–3½" x 60¾" side borders.
- 3–1½"-wide strips for strip sets

From the multicolor print cut

- 1–4¼" x 12½" rectangle for Row A ground
- 1–4¼" x 17½" rectangle for Row B ground
- 1–2¾" x 12½" rectangle for Row C ground
- 6–2¼"-wide strips for binding

From the yellow tone-on-tone print cut

- 3–2"-wide strips for strip sets

Prepare the Appliqué Pieces

1. Following the instructions in Preparing Fused Appliqué on page 110, build the following units on non-stick pressing sheet or parchment paper. Parts of vehicles that will overlap row seam lines cannot be added until after rows are joined.The patterns are found on pages 76-83, the layouts on page 84.
   Note: The layouts can be enlarged and used to arrange appliqué pieces.

Pickup Truck

- 1–Truck Cab B
- 1–Truck Bed
- 2–Wheel B
- 2–Hubcap B
- 1–Bumper
- 1–Headlight B
- 1–Flasher

Cement Truck

- 1–Truck Cab A
- 1–Cement Truck Bed
- 3–Wheel A
- 3–Hubcap A
- 1–Cement Truck Hopper
- 1–Cement Truck Hopper Detail
- 1–Headlight A

Tow Truck

- 1–Truck Cab C
- 1–Truck Bed
- 2–Wheel B
- 2–Hubcap B
- 1–Headlight B
- 1–Flasher
- 1–Box B
- 1–Tow Truck Arm
- 1–Pivot Arm

Dump Truck

- 1–Truck Cab A
- 1–Dump Truck Bed
- 3–Wheel A
- 3–Hubcap A
- 1–Dump Truck Container
- 1–Dump Truck Top
- 1–Headlight A

Flatbed Truck

- 1–Truck Cab B
- 1–Flatbed Truck Bed
- 2–Wheel B
- 2–Hubcap B
- 1–Headlight B
- 1–Box A
- 1–Box B

Car

- 1–Car
- 2–Wheel C
- 2–Hubcap C
- 1–Bumper
- 1–Headlight B
- 1–Taillight

Backhoe

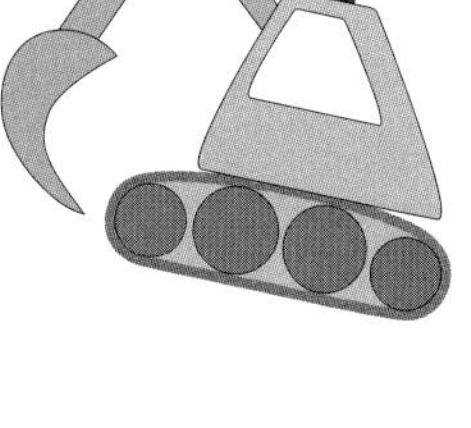

- 1–Backhoe Cab
- 2–Wheel B
- 2–Wheel C
- 1–Flasher
- 1–Earth Mover Track
- 1–Pivot Arm
- 1–Dump Truck Bed
- 1–Scoop

Bulldozer

- 1–Bulldozer Cab
- 2–Wheel B
- 2 –Wheel C
- 1–Flasher
- 1 –Earth Mover Track
- 1–Pivot Arm
- 1–Box A
- 1–Blade

Dirt

- 2–Dirt

Letters

- Use the Alphabet Puzzle Patterns on pages 68-71 to make the letters to spell CONSTRUCTION ZONE.

2. Apply 1–$7\frac{1}{2}$" x 20" rectangle of fusible web to each blue print fat quarter, then from each cut 3–$2\frac{1}{4}$" x 20" rectangles for roads.

Assemble Inner Borders

1. Sew 3 yellow 2"-wide strips and 3 black 1½"-wide strips to make a strip set.
2. Sub cut strip set into 2"-wide 60° diagonal segments by placing 60° line on ruler on one edge of strip set. Make cut along edge of ruler. Then cut 10–2"-wide segments.

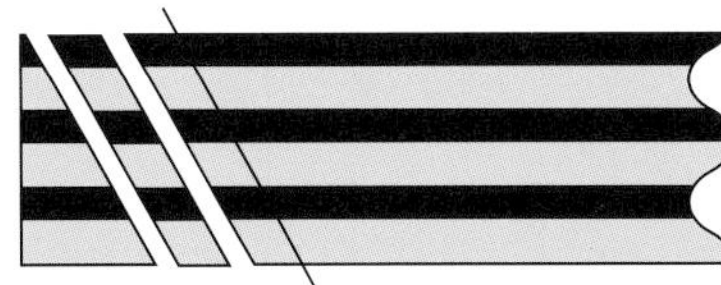

3. Join 5 segments to make top inner border. Trim border to 41½"-long.

4. Repeat for bottom inner border.

Assemble Outer Borders

1. Position the letters CONSTRUCTION on top outer border. Center the letters on the border; X marks the center.

2. Position the letters ZONE on bottom outer border. Center the letters on the border; X marks the center.

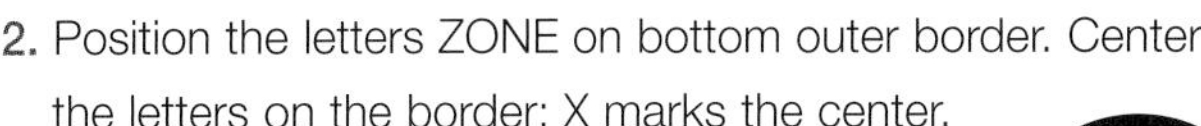

3. Fuse the letters in place.
4. Stitch the letters with a satin zigzag stitch using matching thread.
5. Trim borders to 41½".

Assemble the Rows

The quilt center is made in vertical rows (A, B, and C). The roads and most of the vehicles are fused and stitched to each background row before joining rows.

1. Sew each multicolor ground rectangle to bottom of appropriate white print row rectangle.

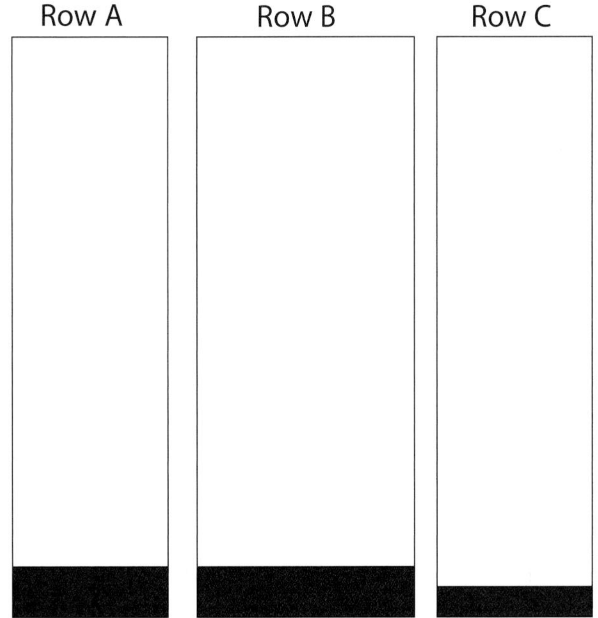

2. Position road rectangles as shown below and on page 22.

- Starting at top of Row A background, place first road rectangle at an angle 10" from top of background on left side and 11½" from top of background on right side. Place second road rectangle at an angle 23¾" from top of background on left side and 25¼" from top of background on right side. Place third road rectangle at an angle 37½" from top of background on left side and 39" from top of background on right side.

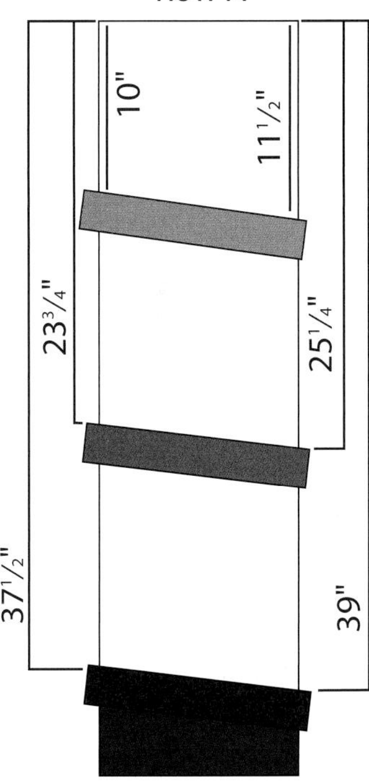

- Starting at top of Row B background, place first road rectangle straight across background 11½" from top of background. Place second road rectangle straight across background 25¼" from top of background. Place third road rectangle straight across background 39" from top of background.

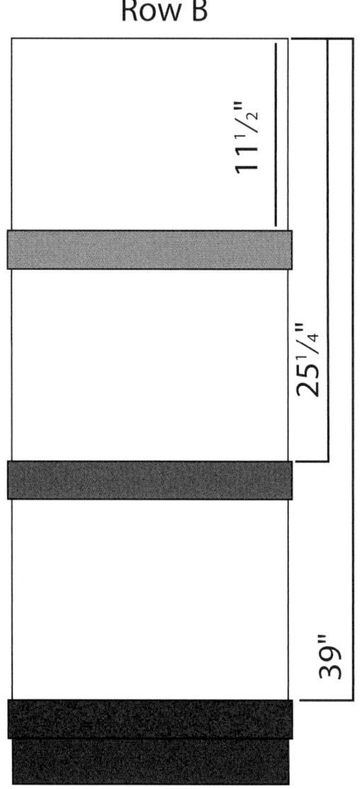

- Starting at top of Row C background, place first road rectangle at an angle 11½" from top of background on left side and 13½" from top of background on right side. Place second road rectangle at an angle 25¼" from top of background on left side and 27¼" from top of background on right side. Place third road rectangle at an angle 39" from top of background on left side and 41" from top of background on right side.

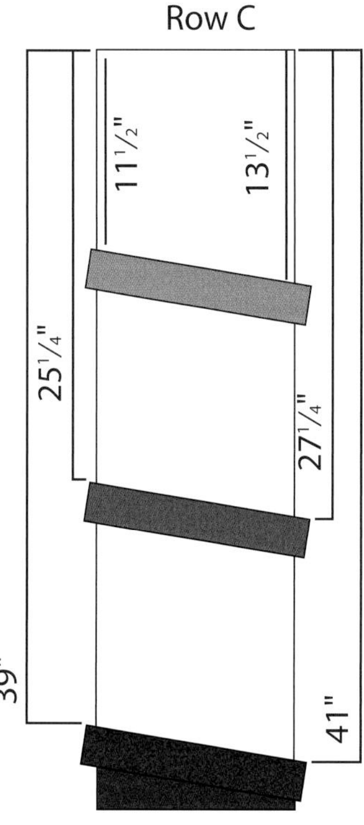

3. Fuse the roads in place.

4. Stitch the roads with a fine zigzag stitch using matching thread.

5. Trim the roads even with edges of row backgrounds.

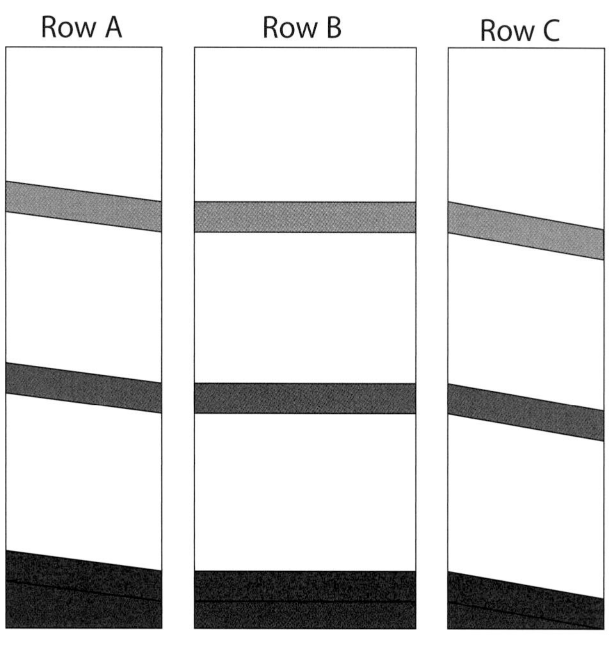

Stitch the Appliqué

1. Position vehicles and partial vehicles on each row and fuse in place.

2. Stitch the appliqué with a fine zigzag stitch, page 116, using matching thread. Leave open edges on the tow truck bar, car front bumper and backhoe bar for inserting parts later. Stitch the edge of the track on the back hoe and bulldozer with a decorative satin stitch, if desired.

Assemble the Quilt

1. Join into rows to complete quilt center.
2. Position remaining vehicle parts that overlap seams. Fuse in place.

3. Stitch the appliqué with a fine zigzag stitch using matching thread.
4. Sew the top and bottom inner borders to the quilt center, being careful not to stretch since these borders have bias edges.
5. Sew the top and bottom outer borders to the quilt center. Sew the side outer borders to the quilt.

Finish the Quilt

1. Cut the backing fabric into 2–1½ yard lengths; join lengthwise.
2. Layer the quilt top, batting, and backing.
3. Refer to Quilting Appliqué on page 126 and quilt as desired.
4. Trim the excess batting and backing to straighten the edges and square the corners.
5. Stitch together the multicolor print 2¼"-wide strips with diagonal seams to make a continuous strip. Use to bind the quilt.

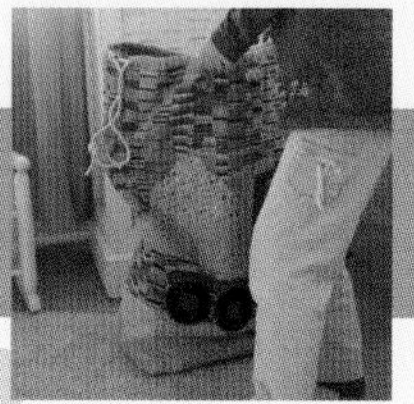

Drawstring Toy Bag

finished size: 11" x 21" x 7"

This nifty drawstring bag with the dump truck appliqué from Construction Zone holds a lot of gear. The truck-themed design just might have kids thinking it's fun to put their toys away.

MATERIALS

Bag Body
- ½ yard multicolor print

Bag Bottom, Lining, and Drawstring Casing
- 1½ yards green print

Appliqué
- Fat quarters and scraps of assorted prints in red, gold, green, and black for vehicle

Paper-backed Fusible Web
- ⅔ yard

Lightweight Quilt Batting
- 28" x 40" piece of quilt batting

Cotton Cord
- 3 yards of ¼"-diameter braided cord

- 1–7" x 11" piece of stiff cardboard or lightweight plastic for bottom insert

Fabric suggestions are 40"-42" wide.

Fat quarter = 18" x 20".

Sew all patchwork seams with a ¼" seam allowance.

Follow manufacturer's directions for using paper-backed fusible web.

Cut the Quilt Pieces

From the multicolor print cut

- 1–16" x 36½" rectangle for bag body

From the green print cut

- 1–8½" x 36½" rectangle for bag bottom
- 1–3" x 36½" rectangle for facing
- 2–3½" x 34½" rectangles for drawstring casings
- 1–26" x 40" rectangle for lining
- 2–8" x 12" rectangles for bottom insert

Prepare the Appliqué Pieces

1. Following the instructions in Preparing Fused Appliqué on page 110, make the dump truck or desired vehicle. Build the truck on non-stick pressing sheet or parchment paper. The patterns are found on pages 76-83.

Assemble Bag Body

1. Sew bag bottom rectangle to bag body rectangle. Press seam toward bottom rectangle. Top stitch ⅛" from seam.

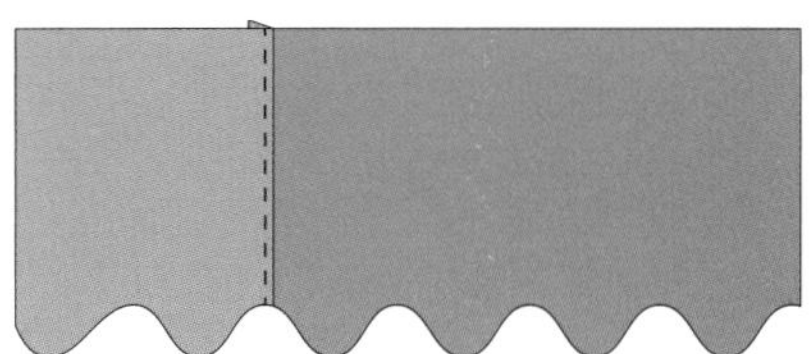

2. Appliqué desired construction vehicle to bag, positioning the wheels about ½" onto the bag bottom and at least ½" away from side.

3. Layer bag body, batting, and lining.
4. Refer to Quilting Appliqué on page 126 and quilt as desired.
5. Trim the excess batting and lining to straighten the edges and square the corners.

6. Fold quilted bag in half with right sides together. Mark the fold using a hand basting stitch. This line will be used as a reference later.

7. Stitch the side and bottom of the bag. Zigzag or overcast the seams.

8. Carefully cut 3¼" squares from each side of the bottom.

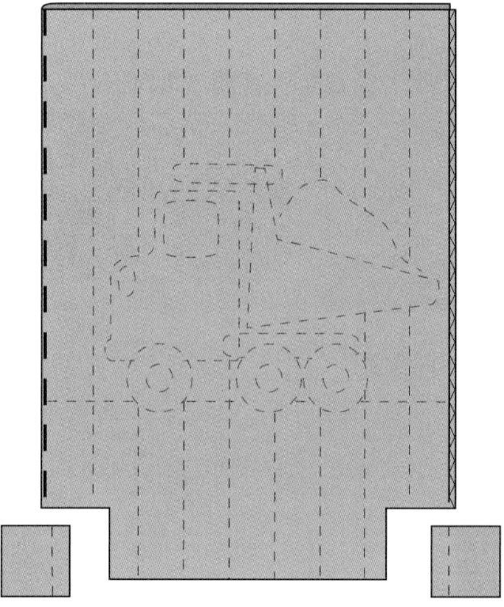

9. Fold bag at the bottom, aligning bottom seam with side seam. Stitch to form bottom corner. Repeat on the other side, lining up the bottom seam with the basting line.

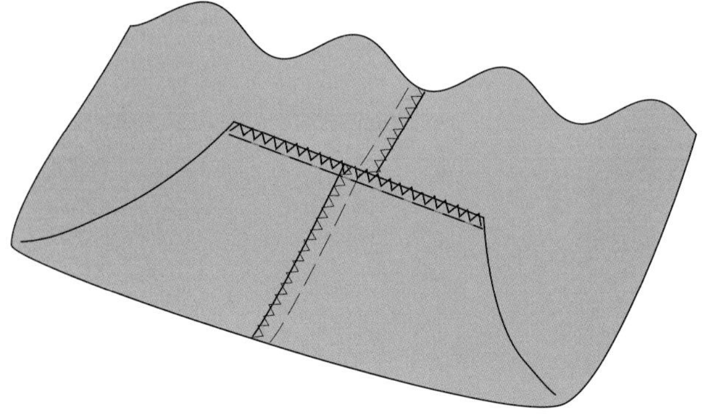

10. Turn the bag right side out.

Casing

1. Join ends of 1 casing rectangle with right sides together. Press seam allowances open.

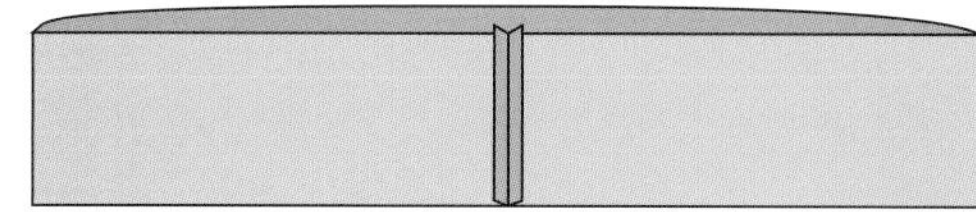

2. Turn casing right side out. Fold casing in half, aligning raw edges, to form a casing tube. Baste edges together. Make 2 casing tubes.

3. Pin casing tubes to right side of top of bag. Center each tube between side seam and basting line.

4. Join ends of facing rectangle to form a continuous strip. Press up ½" of one long edge of strip to the wrong side. Stitch close to edge to hem facing.

5. With right sides together, pin the raw edge of facing to the top of bag.

6. Stitch through all layers around top of bag, encasing the casing tubes.

7. Press seam toward facing. Top stitch about 1/8" from the seam through facing and seam allowance only.

8. Press facing to the inside of bag. Hand stitch facing to lining.

Finish the Bag

1. Cut 2–54"-lengths of cord. Starting at one side, thread 1 cord through 1 casing then the other. Tie the ends with an overhand knot. Thread the remaining cord through the 2 casings in the opposite direction. Tie ends with an overhand knot.

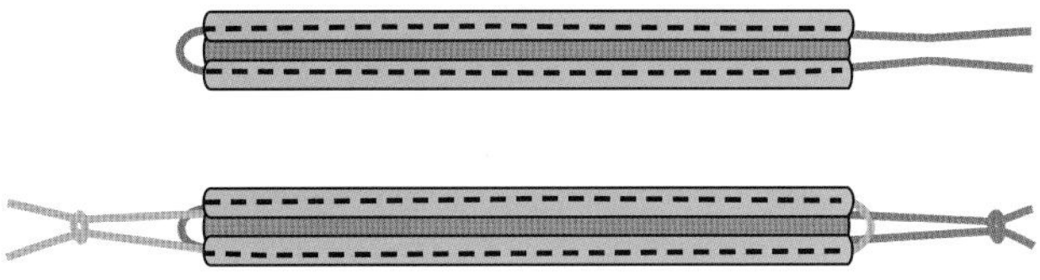

2. Measure bottom of bag. Cut insert cardboard rectangle this size. Lay the cardboard on the wrong side of one of the insert fabrics and mark a line about 1/8" from cardboard. Stitch on this line on the 2 long sides and one end. Turn right side out. Insert cardboard into fabric sleeve. Whipstitch last seam. Insert into bottom of bag; tack in place. Remove insert before laundering bag.

be creative

Construction Zone

Butterfly Toy Bag

Construct this Drawstring Toy Bag for the princess in your life using butterfly and flower motifs from Paisley Princess on page 40. Use a 1" grosgrain ribbon instead of cording for the drawstrings.

The Bugs are Buzzing

Convert Construction Zone roads to backyard paths and fly zones. Mix and match the bug patterns to make these insects or have fun and design your own motifs with input from your kids. Download bug patterns and layouts at www.landauerpub.com.

Construction Zone

Using Decorative Stitches for Added Texture

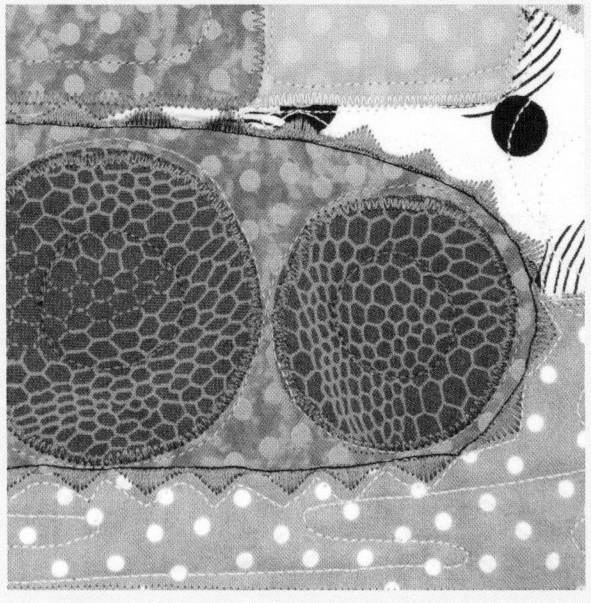

To give texture realism to the backhoe and bulldozer, use a decorative satin stitch that forms triangles or spikes. Position the points outward toward the road bed.

To make the tires appear to have tread sew the stitch shown, a similar decorative stitch, or a wide buttonhole stitch around the edges using gray thread. Stitch around the hubcap using the same stitch but with the points aiming out as for spokes.

Talk to kids about safety

Many construction vehicles are very big and high off the ground. The driver may have trouble seeing a child so be sure to catch the driver's eye before crossing in front. Never walk behind a vehicle unless you have talked with the driver and he is aware you are there.

Drivers Needed

Find some fun fabric with kid, workman or animal prints. Fuse, cut out, and appliqué the motifs to appear as drivers inside the equipment vehicles.

Talk to kids about safety

Ever hear a construction vehicle beeping? That is a signal it is backing up.

For a Hard Hat Look

Instead of dotted fabrics use a combination of plaids, shirt prints, and solids for Construction Zone background and equipment.

Flower Power

finished size: 42" x 42"

Use your child's favorite colors in a variety of prints or batiks to make this retro-looking quilt come to life.

MATERIALS

Appliqué and Pieced Border
- 7 fat quarters in assorted fabrics in violet, green, turquoise, and blue prints

Background
- 1⅛ yards white print

Binding
- ½ yard green print

Backing
- 2¾ yards backing fabric

Paper-Backed Fusible Web
- 1¾ yards

Quilt Batting
- 48" x 48" piece of quilt batting

Fabric suggestions are 40"-42" wide.
Fat quarter = 18" x 20".

Sew all patchwork seams with a ¼" seam allowance.

Follow manufacturer's directions for using paper-backed fusible web.

Cut the Quilt Pieces

From background fabric cut
- 4–18½" squares

From each fat quarter cut
- 4–1½"-wide strips from the 20", the widest side, of the fat quarter

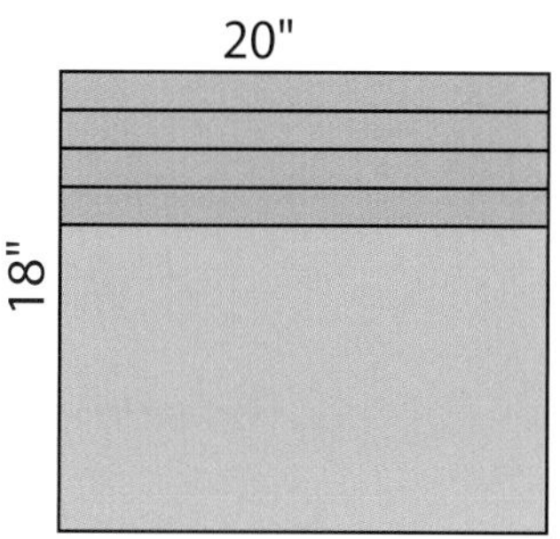

From remainder of 1 fat quarter
- 4–3½" squares for border corners

Note: Remainders of fat quarters will be used for rounded squares (templates A-E)

From binding fabric cut
- 1–1½"-wide strip. Cut strip in half to make 2–1½" x 20" strips.
- 5–2¼"-wide strips for binding

Prepare the Appliqué Pieces

Following the instructions in Preparing Fused Appliqué on page 110 make the following appliqué pieces using remainders of fat quarters and binding fabric. The patterns are found on page 85 and page 87.

- 5 sets of Rounded Squares
- 4 solid Rounded Squares A

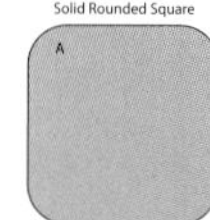

- 4 Flower A

- 4 Flower B

Each part of rounded squares sets will be used. Carefully cut sets apart after fusible web is applied. Start on one straight side and make a slit with seam ripper or rotary cutter. Finish cutting rounded squares sets with scissors.

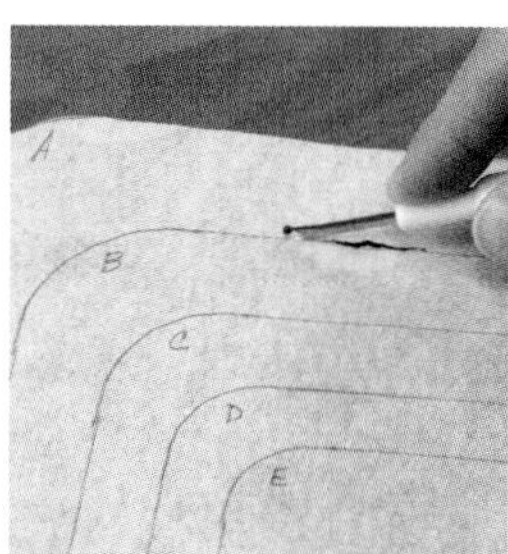

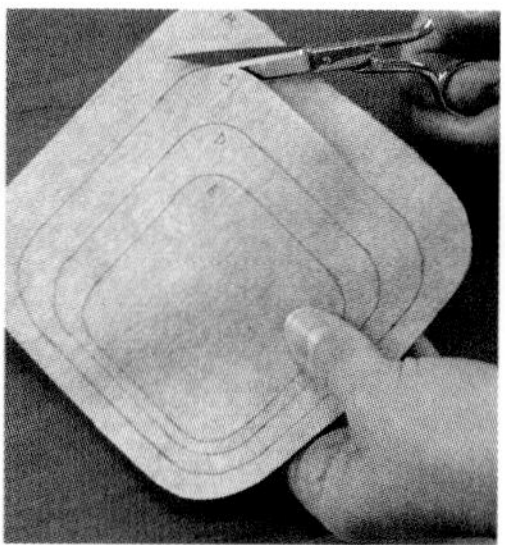

1. Select a set of rounded squares (A-E) in assorted colors and set aside.

2. Divide remaining rounded squares and arrange randomly on the 4 background squares. Leave space for the set aside squares to be placed after background squares are sewn together. Position flowers on A squares. Fuse in place.

Note: Take a photo at this stage as a reminder of where to fuse the set aside rounded squares later.

Stitch the Appliqué

1. Stitch the rounded squares with a fine or satin zigzag stitch, page 116 and page 118, using matching thread.

2. Stitch the flowers using decorative machine stitches, if desired.

Assemble the Quilt

1. Join 4 appliquéd background squares; press seams open.

2. Arrange remaining rounded squares over background seams. Fuse in place; stitch using the the same stitch as the other rounded squares and matching thread to complete quilt center.

Assemble Inner Borders and the Quilt

1. Sew 6 assorted $1\frac{1}{2}$"-wide strips to make a strip set. Make 5 strip sets. Sub cut each strip set into 5–$3\frac{1}{2}$"-wide segments (There will be 1 extra).

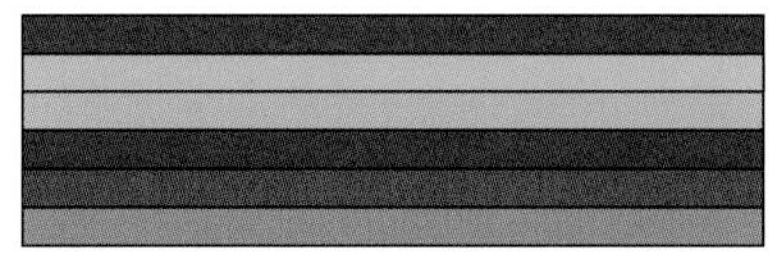

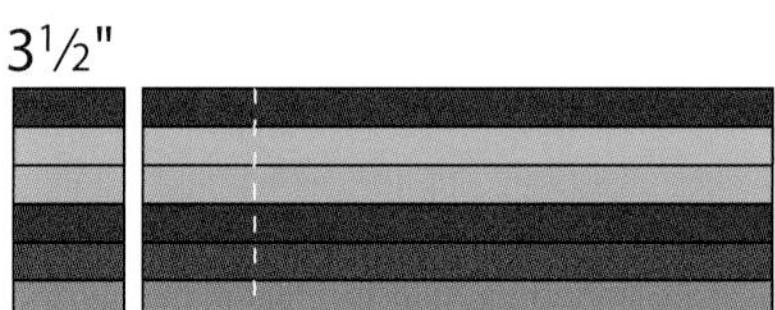

2. Join 6 assorted segments to make 1 inner border. Make 4 inner borders.

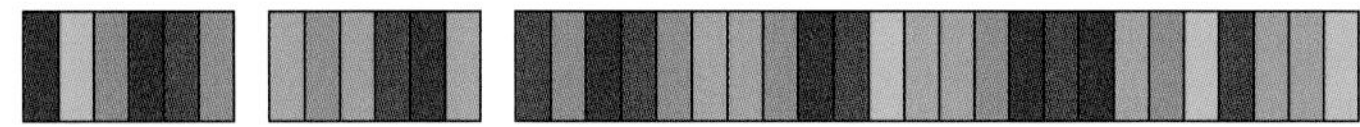

3. Sew 2 inner borders to opposite sides of quilt center.

4. Sew 1–3½" square to each end of remaining inner borders. Sew borders to top and bottom of quilt.

Finish the Quilt

1. Cut the backing fabric into 2–1⅜ yard lengths; join lengthwise.

2. Layer the quilt top, batting, and backing.

3. Refer to Quilting Appliqué on page 126 and quilt as desired.

4. Trim the excess batting and backing to straighten the edges and square the corners.

5. Stitch together the 5–2¼"-wide strips with diagonal seams to make a continuous strip. Use to bind the quilt.

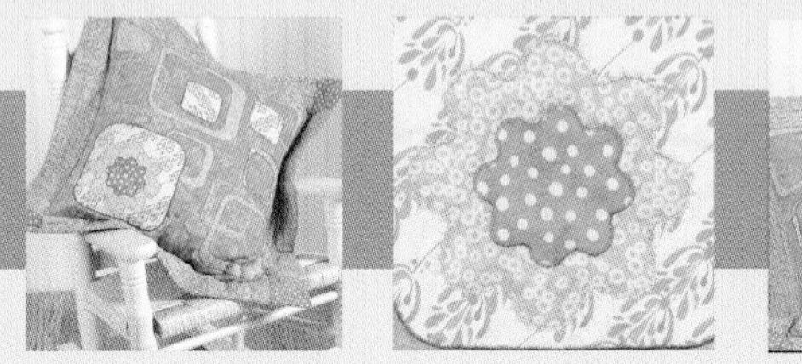

Flower Power Square Pillow

finished size: 24" x 24"

This large pillow can provide the decorative finish to a couch or bed. It is also perfect for tossing on the floor for extra seating.

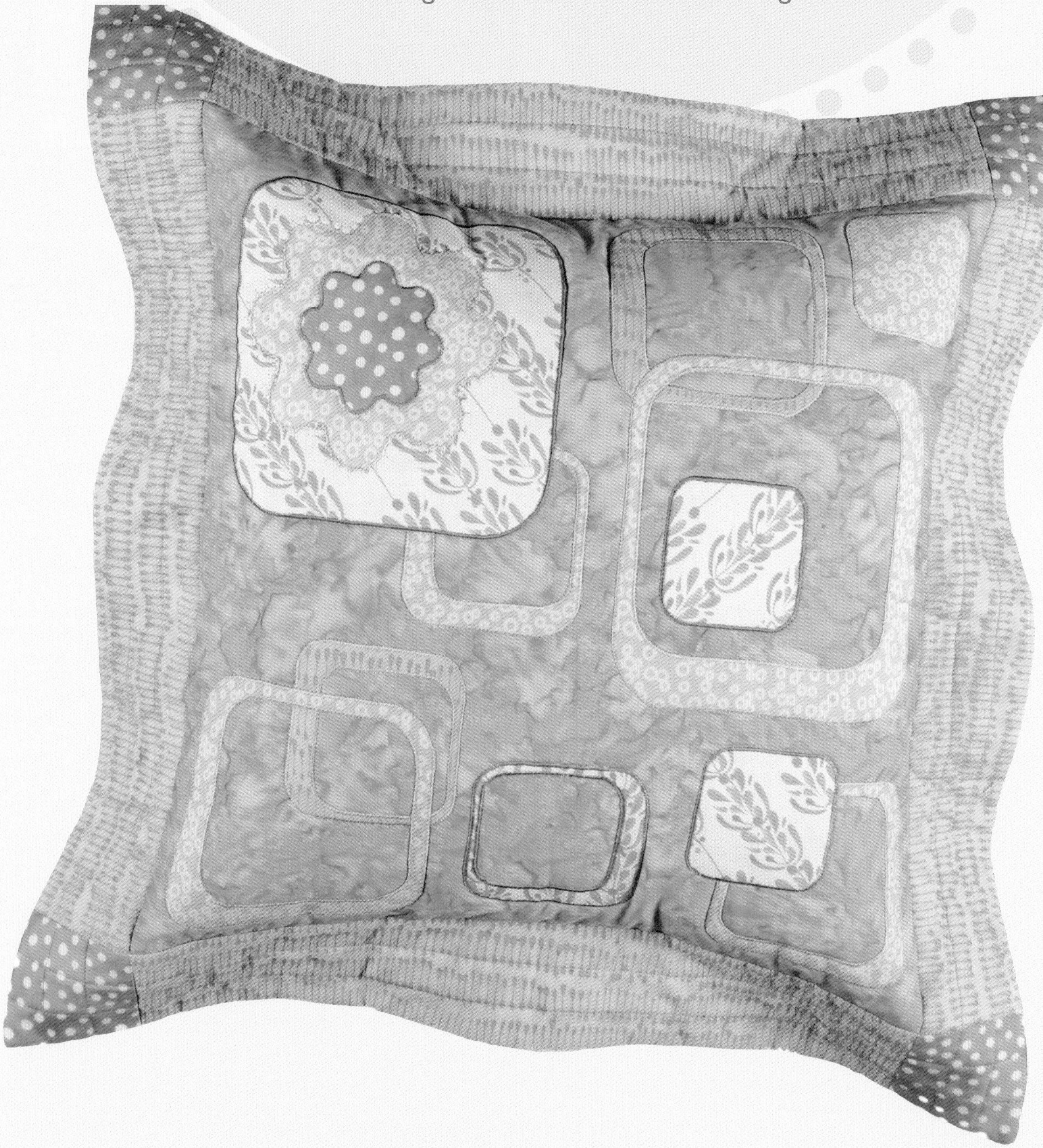

MATERIALS

Pillow Top Background
- 5/8 yard turquoise print

Border and Back
- 2 3/8 yards gold stripe
- 12" square turquoise dot

Appliqué
- 1 fat quarter gold tone-on-tone print
- 1 fat quarter white print
- Remainders from border fabrics

Lining
- 30" x 30" piece of muslin

Paper-Backed Fusible Web
- 1 yard

Quilt Batting
- 30" x 30" piece of quilt batting

Pillow Insert
- 18" square

Fabric suggestions are 40"-42" wide.
Fat quarter = 18" x 20".

Sew all patchwork seams
with a 1/4" seam allowance.

Follow manufacturer's directions for
using paper-backed fusible web.

Cut the Pillow Pieces

From turquoise print cut
- 1–18 1/2" background square

From gold stripe cut
- 4–3 1/2" x 18 1/2" borders
- 2–24 1/2" x 30" rectangles for pillow back

From turquoise dot cut
- 4–3 1/2" border squares

Prepare the Appliqué Pieces

Following the instructions in Preparing Fused Appliqué on page 110, make the following appliqué pieces. The patterns are found on page 85 and page 87.

Gold tone-on-tone print
- 1 set of Rounded Squares
- 1 Flower A

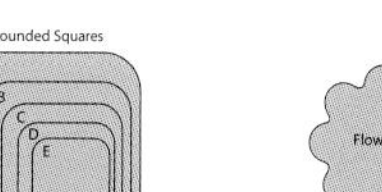

White print
- 1 solid Rounded Square A
- 2 solid Rounded Square E
- 1 hollow Rounded Square D

Gold stripe
- 1 hollow Rounded Square C
- 1 hollow Rounded Square D

Turquoise dot
- 1 Flower B

Each part of the rounded squares set will be used. Carefully cut set apart after fusible web is applied. Start on one straight side and make a slit with seam ripper or rotary cutter. Finish cutting rounded square sets with scissors.

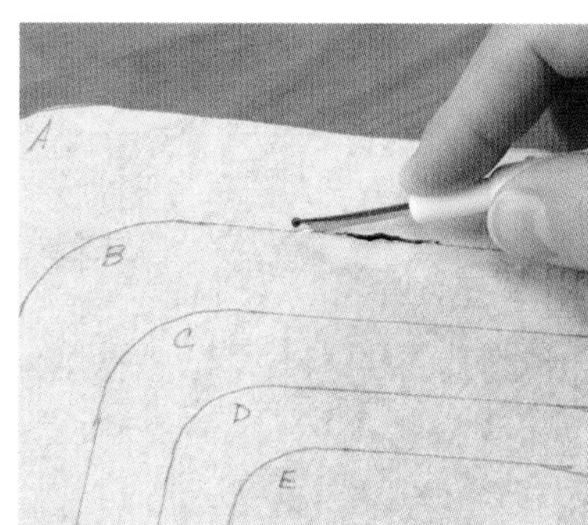

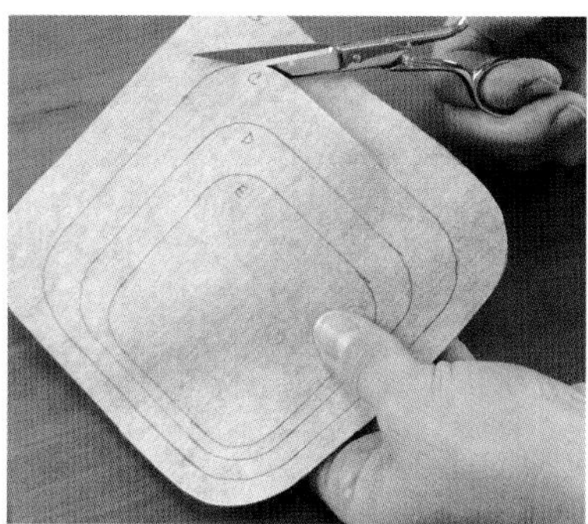

1. Arrange appliqué pieces on the background square. Fuse in place.

Stitch the Appliqué

1. Stitch the rounded squares with a satin zigzag stitch, page 118, using matching thread.
2. Stitch the flower using decorative machine stitches, if desired.

Assemble the Pillow Top

1. Sew 1 border to opposite sides of pillow top center.
2. Sew 1 border square to each end of remaining borders. Sew borders to top and bottom of pillow top.

3. Layer the pillow top, batting, and lining.
4. Refer to Quilting Appliqué on page 126 and quilt as desired.
5. Trim the excess batting and lining to straighten the edges and square the corners.

Finish the Pillow

1. Fold each back rectangle in half with wrong sides facing.
2. Lay the back rectangles together overlapping the folded edges to make a $24\frac{1}{2}$" square.

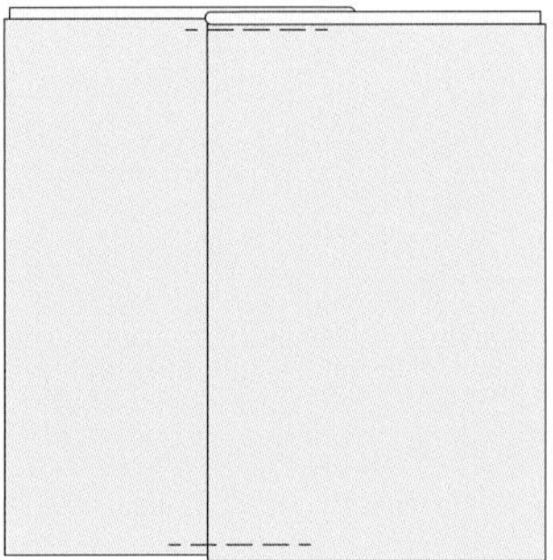

3. Baste across the overlap to hold while joining to pillow top.
4. With right sides together lay the pillow top on the pillow back. Trim the back to the size of the front. (The quilting may have made the top shrink slightly.)
5. Sew around all four sides with $\frac{1}{4}$" seam allowance. Trim the corners.
6. Turn right side out. Lightly press the outside edge and corners. Stitch in the ditch between the background and the border all the way around the top.
7. Insert pillow.

Flower Power

Pink Power

Make this variation of Flower Power into a larger quilt by choosing 10 pink, red, and orange fat quarters for the borders and appliqué.

1. Cut 5–1½" strips for the border strip sets from each fat quarter.
2. Following the instructions in Preparing Fused Appliqué on page 110, make the following appliqué pieces. The patterns are found on page 85 and page 87.

- 7 sets of Rounded Squares
- 6 solid Rounded Squares A
- 6 Flower A
- 6 Flower B

3. Cut 4–3½" squares.
4. Use 6–20½" x 18½" rectangles for the background.

Peace Pillow or Quilt

Make a floor pillow or Flower Power quilt using the nested circles and peace symbol found on page 86, instead of the rounded squares and flower B.

Place Mat

finished size: 13" x 18"

Make this place mat with a favorite kid print for the appliqué circles or feature the print as the background with solid color circle appliqués on top. Or, use a motif from Construction Zone or Paisley Princess.

MATERIALS

Appliqué
1 fat quarter kid print

Background
1 fat quarter OR ½ yard green tone-on-tone print

Side Border
1 fat quarter stripe OR ¼ yard vertical stripe OR ½ yard horizontal stripe

Backing
1 fat quarter

Quilt Batting
18" x 20" piece of quilt batting

Fabric suggestions are 40"-42" wide.
Fat quarter = 18" x 20".

Sew all patchwork seams with a ¼" seam allowance.

Follow manufacturer's directions for using paper-backed fusible web.

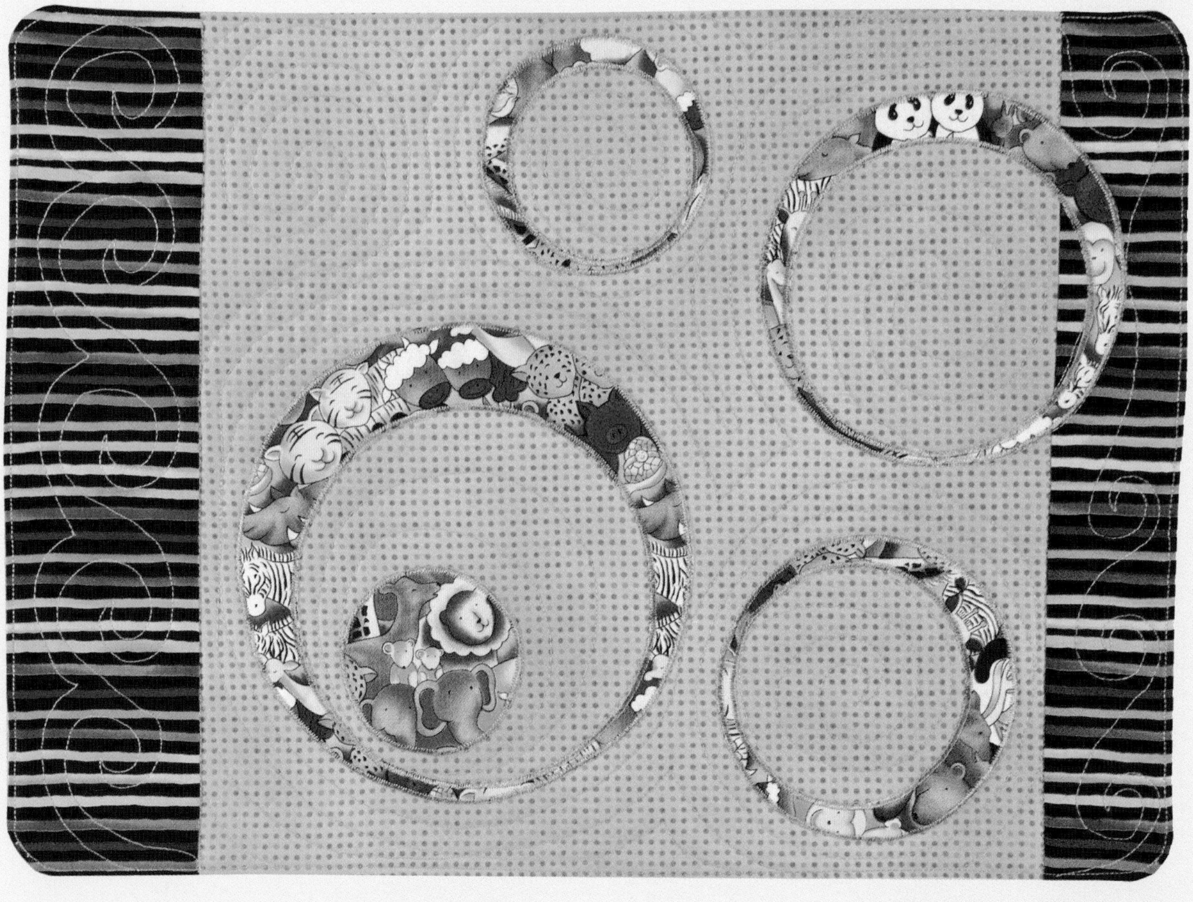

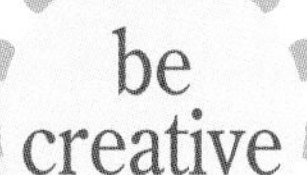

Cut the Quilt Pieces

From background fabric cut

1–13½" square.

From side border fabric cut

1–3½" x 13½" rectangle

1–2½" x 13½" rectangle

Prepare the Appliqué Pieces

1. Following the instructions in Preparing Fused Appliqué on page 110, make 1 set nested circles from kid print fabric appliqué pieces. The pattern is found on page 86.
2. Each part of the nested circle set will be used. Carefully cut set apart after fusible web is applied. Make a slit with seam ripper or rotary cutter and finish cutting nested circle set with scissors.

Assemble the Place Mat

1. Sew the 3½" x 13½" rectangle to the left side of the background square. Sew the 2½" x 13½" rectangle to the right side of the background square to make the place mat.

2. Arrange the appliqué pieces on the pieced place mat. Fuse in place.

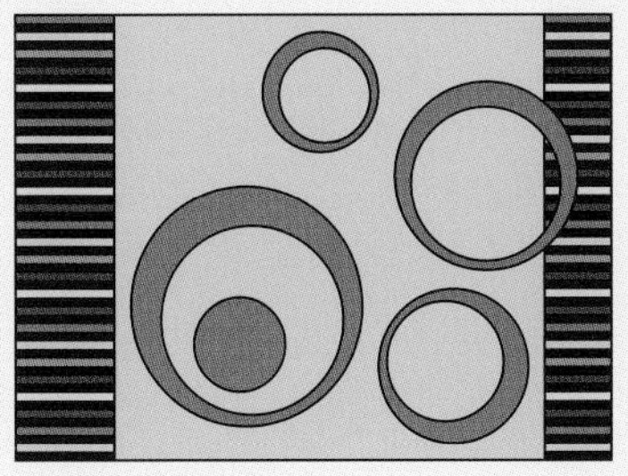

Stitch the Appliqué

1. Stitch the circles with a satin zigzag stitch, page 118, using contrasting thread.

Finish the Place Mat

1. Layer batting, backing fabric (right side up), and place mat top (wrong side up).
2. Sew around all four sides with ¼" seam allowance, rounding corners if desired. See photo on page 17. Leave a 5" opening on one side for turning.
3. Trim backing and batting even with edges of place mat top. Clip or trim corners.
4. Turn right side out. Lightly press the outside edge and corners. Hand stitch the opening closed.
5. Top stitch around the place mat ⅛" in from the edge. Quilt as desired.

Paisley Princess

finished size 42" x 55"

A delight for any little princess to sleep under.

MATERIALS

Background and Border

- 1¼ yards multicolor print for border and binding
- ½ yard light violet stripe for princess background
- ¾ yard green print for paisley block and butterfly block background
- ⅜ yard light violet print for flower block background
- 1 fat quarter dark violet print for tiara background
- ¼ yard turquoise print for magic wand background
- ¼ yard (or 1 fat quarter) medium violet print
- 1 fat quarter violet/green dot
- 1 fat quarter green stripe

Appliqué

- 3 fat quarters in assorted prints in light, medium, and dark violet for princess dress

Note: I used a cotton/silk blend fabric with a slight sheen for the princess dress. If you plan to wash your quilt, be sure to check each fabric's care instructions before using it in your quilt.

- 1 fat quarter violet stripe for magic wand
- Assorted fat quarters and scraps for appliqué pieces (turquoise, violet, green, pink, flesh, and gold)

Backing

- 2¾ yards backing fabric

Paper-Backed Fusible Web

- 2 yards

Quilt Batting

- 48" x 61" piece of quilt batting (or Crib-size batting)

Fabric suggestions are 40"-42" wide.
Fat quarter = 18" x 20".

Sew all patchwork seams with a ¼" seam allowance.

Follow manufacturer's directions for using paper-backed fusible web.

Cut the Quilt Pieces

From the multicolor print cut

- 2–4½" x 34½" top and bottom borders
- 3–4½"-wide strips.
  Join strips, then cut 2–4½" x 55½" side borders.
- 6–2¼" strips for binding

From the light violet stripe cut

- 1–13½" x 24" rectangle for princess block background

From the green print cut

- 1–10½" x 37½" rectangle for paisley block background
- 1–11½" x 13" rectangle for butterfly block background

From the light violet print cut

- 1–10½" x 24½" rectangle for flower block background

From the dark violet print cut

- 1–10" x 20" rectangle for tiara block background

From the turquoise print cut

- 1–4½" x 24½" rectangle for magic wand block background

From the medium violet print cut

- 1–6½" x 11½" rectangle

From the violet/green dot cut

- 1–10½" square
- 1–2½" x 11½" rectangle

From the green stripe cut

- 1–5" x 10" rectangle
- 1–11½" x 3½" rectangle

Prepare the Appliqué Pieces

1. Following the instructions in Preparing Fused Appliqué on page 110, build the following units on non-stick pressing sheet or parchment paper. The patterns are found on pages 87-91, the layouts on page 92.

   Note: The layouts can be enlarged and used to arrange appliqué pieces and mark detail lines.

Princess block

- 1–Dress Bodice
- 1–Upper Skirt
- 2–Lower Skirt
- 1–Face
- 1–Hair
- 1–Arm A
- 1–Arm B
- 1–Tiara
- 1–Star B
- 1–Wand

Paisley block

- 6–Paisley A
- 6–Paisley Center A

Tiara block

- 1–Paisley A
- 1–Paisley B
- 2–Paisley Center A
- 2–Paisley Center B
- 1–Tiara Base
- 1–Heart

Butterfly block

- 2–Paisley B
- 2–Paisley Center B
- 1–Butterfly Accent
- 1–Butterfly Body
- 1–Butterfly Head

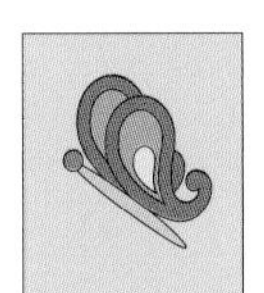

Flower block

- 2–Flower A
- 2–Flower B
- 1–Paisley A
- 1–Paisley B
- 1–Paisley Center A
- 1–Paisley Center B
- 1–Butterfly Body
- 1–Butterfly Head

Magic Wand block

- 1–Star A
- Wand: From violet stripe fat quarter cut a bias strip 1¼" x 20". Press a 1" x 19" piece of fusible web to the strip. Cut a ¾" x 18" rectangle for the wand.

Stitch the Appliqué

1. Arrange the appliqué units and pieces on the background rectangles referring to the photograph on page 40 and the diagrams in Assemble the Quilt. Fuse in place.
2. Stitch the appliqué with fine or satin zigzag stitch, page 116 and page 118, or decorative stitches using matching or contrasting thread as shown below.
3. Add the smile and eyes to the princess following suggestions in "be creative" on page 48.

Assemble the Quilt

1. Lay out the blocks and remaining background pieces. Join into sections; join sections to make the quilt center.
2. Sew the top and bottom borders to the quilt center. Sew the side borders to the quilt.

Finish the Quilt

1. Cut the backing fabric into 2–1⅜ yard lengths; join lengthwise.
2. Layer the quilt top, batting, and backing.
3. Refer to Quilting Appliqué on page 126 and quilt as desired.
4. Trim the excess batting and backing to straighten the edges and square the corners.
5. Stitch together the 6–2¼"-wide strips with diagonal seams to make a continuous strip. Use to bind the quilt.

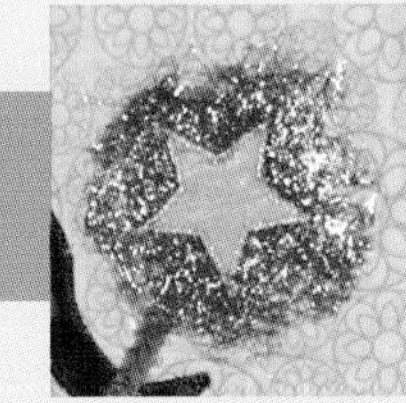

Bedazzled Princess

finished size: 28" x 32½"

Glam-up your princess with ribbons, beads, and crystal embellishments. The perfect wallhanging for any little girl's room.

MATERIALS

Background and Border

- 3/4 yard green print for border and binding
- 1/2 yard light green print for princess background
- 1/2 yard pink print for butterfly block background and left inner border
- 1 fat quarter violet stripe for flower block background
- 1/4 yard (or 1 fat quarter) multicolor print
- 1/4 yard (or 1 fat quarter) dark pink print

Appliqué

- 3 fat quarters in assorted prints in light, medium, and dark violet for princess dress
- 10" squares and assorted scraps for appliqué pieces (flesh and hair, green, fuchsia, orange, gold and violet including lamé fabrics for crown and star)
- 9" of 1/4"-wide ribbon for wand
- Assorted beads, crystals, Angelina for embellishing

Backing

- 1 1/4 yards backing fabric

Paper-Backed Fusible Web

- 1 1/4 yard

Quilt Batting

- 36" x 44" piece of quilt batting

Fabric suggestions are 40"-42" wide.
Fat quarter = 18" x 20".

Sew all patchwork seams with a 1/4" seam allowance.

Follow manufacturer's directions for using paper-backed fusible web.

Cut the Background Pieces

From the green print cut

- 2–3 1/2" x 27" side borders
- 2–3 1/2" x 28 1/2" top and bottom borders
- 4–2 1/4" strips for binding

From the light green print cut

- 1–11 1/2" x 23" rectangle for princess block background

From the pink print cut

- 1–10 1/2" x 12" rectangle for butterfly block background
- 1–1 1/2" x 27" strip for left inner border

From the violet stripe cut

- 1–10 1/2" x 7" rectangle for flower block background

From the multicolor print cut

- 1–10 1/2" x 5" rectangle

From the dark pink print cut

- 1–4 1/2" x 21 1/2" rectangle

Prepare the Appliqué Pieces

1. Following the instructions in Preparing Fused Appliqué on page 110, build the following units on non-stick pressing sheet or parchment paper. The patterns are found on pages 87-91, the layouts on page 92.

   Note: The layouts can be enlarged and used to arrange appliqué pieces and mark detail lines.

Princess block

- 1–Dress Bodice
- 1–Upper Skirt
- 2–Lower Skirt
- 1–Face
- 1–Hair
- 1–Arm A
- 1–Arm B
- 1–Tiara
- 1–Star A
- 1–Wand (9"-long piece of 1/4"-wide ribbon)
- 2" circle of pressed Angelina (page 124)

Butterfly block

- 1–Paisley A
- 1–Paisley B
- 1–Paisley Center A
- 1–Paisley Center B
- 2–Butterfly Accent
- 1–Butterfly Body
- 1–Butterfly Head

Flower block

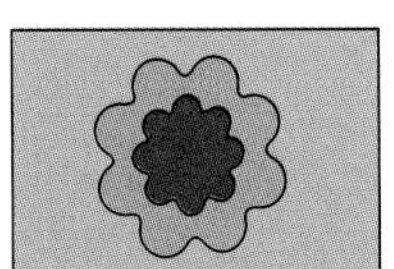

- 1–Flower A
- 1–Flower B

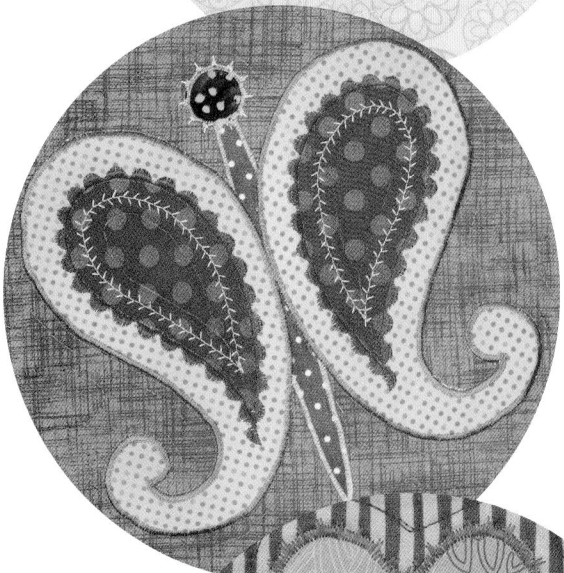

Stitch the Appliqué

1. Arrange the appliqué pieces on the background pieces referring to the photograph on page 44 and the diagrams in Assemble the Quilt. Fuse in place.
2. Stitch the appliqué with fine or satin zigzag stitch, page 116 and page 118, or decorative stitches, as shown, using matching or contrasting thread. Refer to Embellishing and Other Embellishments, pages 120-124, for more embellishing ideas. If using Angelina under the star, set aside star appliqué and Angelina to add after quilting. Add other non-fabric embellishments after quilting and binding.

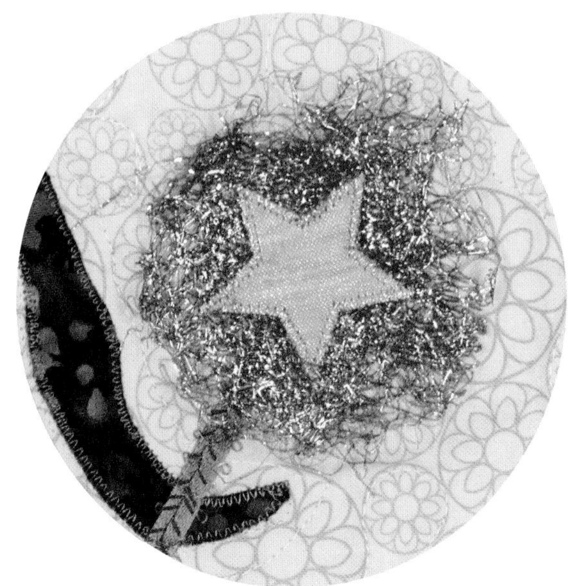

3. Add the smile and eyes to the princess following suggestions in 'be creative" on page 48.

Assemble the Quilt

1. Lay out the blocks and remaining background pieces. Join into sections; join sections to make the quilt center.
2. Sew the side borders to the quilt center. Sew the top and bottom borders to the quilt.

Finish the Quilt

1. Layer the quilt top, batting, and backing.
2. Refer to Quilting Appliqué on page 126 and quilt as desired.
3. Trim the excess batting and backing to straighten the edges and square the corners.
4. Stitch together the 4–2¼"-wide strips with diagonal seams to make a continuous strip. Use to bind the quilt.
5. Add more embellishments to bedazzle the quilt.
   Refer to "be creative" on page 48 and Other Embellishments on pages 122-124 for more details.

Paisley Princess

Adding a Smile

Referring to the directions on page 113, make an overlay of the facial features. Pin at the hairline and stitch with your choice of thread colors. If you prefer not to stitch, add the mouth and eyes with permanent inks or markers such as Fabrico® Markers, Pigma Micron Markers, Sakura Gelly Roll® Pens, and watercolor pencils which are permanent when heat set. Keep in mind that inks and markers may fade a bit with repeated washing.

Using Decorative Stitches

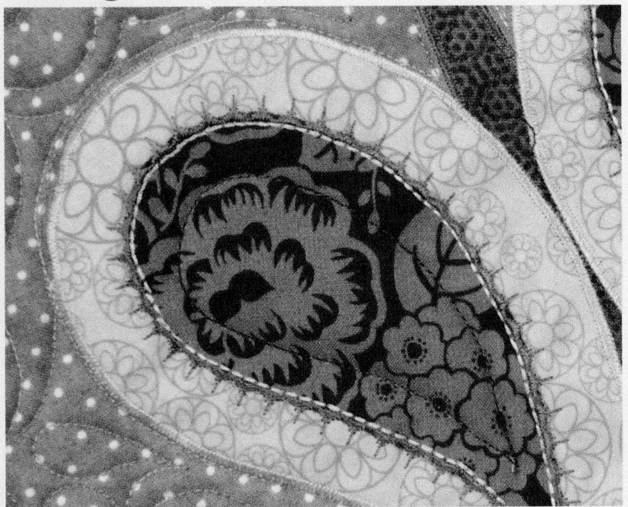

Add triple stitching to outline a shape. This can add emphasis to a line by using a darker or contrasting color.

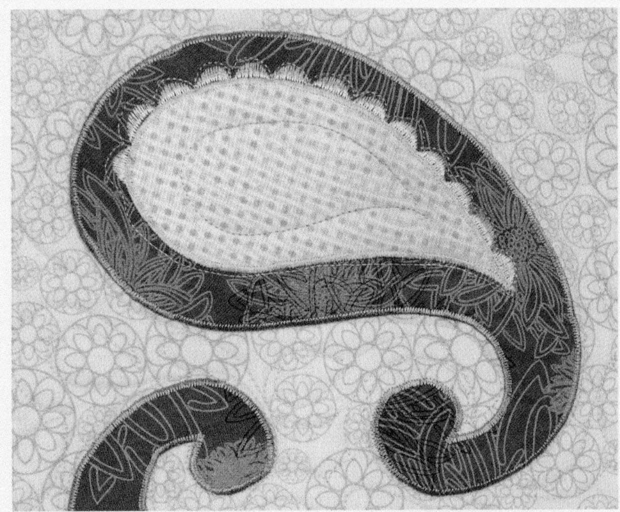

On the row of paisley shapes use a decorative scallop stitch to outline the outer curve of the inner shape.

Paisley Princess

Interior Decorating

Design a princess-themed room by adding paisley motifs to purchased curtains. You could also appliqué a butterfly to a purchased pillow cover that zips off for easy cleaning.

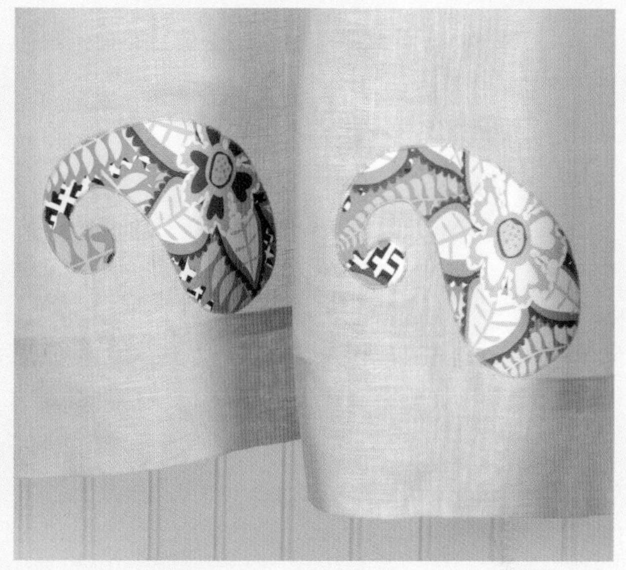

For Your Princess

To personalize the Paisley Princess quilt or Bedazzled Princess wallhanging use "princess" or the recipient's name using the alphabet letters pattern found on pages 72-73. You can also use a row of hearts in one of the rectangles, as shown in the illustration.

Rainbow Twist

finished size: 40" x 50"

Batiks, with their blending qualities and vivid colors, work well for this twirl of rainbow colors.

MATERIALS

Block Fabric

- 4 fat quarters yellow print fabric
- 4 fat quarters violet print fabric
- 4 fat quarters turquoise print fabric
- 4 fat quarters green print fabric
- 4 fat quarters peach print fabric

Binding Fabric

- 3/8 yard multicolor print

Backing

- 1 5/8 yards backing fabric
  (If a longarm machine is to be used for quilting, you will need 2 3/4 yards for a pieced back.)

Paper-Backed Fusible Web

- 1 1/4 yards

Quilt Batting

- 46" x 56" piece of quilt batting
  (or Crib-size batting)

Fabric suggestions are 40"-42" wide.
Fat quarter = 18" x 20".

Sew all patchwork seams
with a 1/4" seam allowance.

Follow manufacturer's directions for
using paper-backed fusible web.

Cut the Quilt Pieces

From yellow fat quarters cut

- 10–5 7/8" squares
- 12–5 1/2" squares

From violet fat quarters cut

- 10–5 7/8" squares
- 12–5 1/2" squares

From turquoise fat quarters cut

- 7–5 7/8" squares
- 18–5 1/2" squares

From green fat quarters cut

- 7–5 7/8" squares
- 18–5 1/2" squares

From peach fat quarters cut

- 6–5 7/8" squares
- 20–5 1/2" squares

From binding fabric cut

- 5–2 1/4"-wide strips

Make the Triangle-Square Blocks

1. Select pairs of 5 7/8" squares in the following combinations:

- 7 violet/turquoise
- 7 green/yellow
- 3 yellow/peach
- 3 violet/peach

Note: For a scrappy look, do not use identical pairs of fabrics. For example, match 7 different violet squares with 7 different turquoise squares; match 7 different green squares with 7 different yellow squares, and so on.

2. Draw a diagonal line across wrong side of one square in each pair.

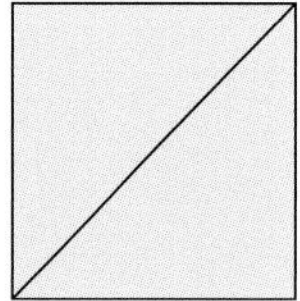

3. Stitch $\frac{1}{4}$" from drawn line on both sides. Cut on drawn line. Press open to reveal triangle-square blocks. Press seam allowances to the darker fabric.

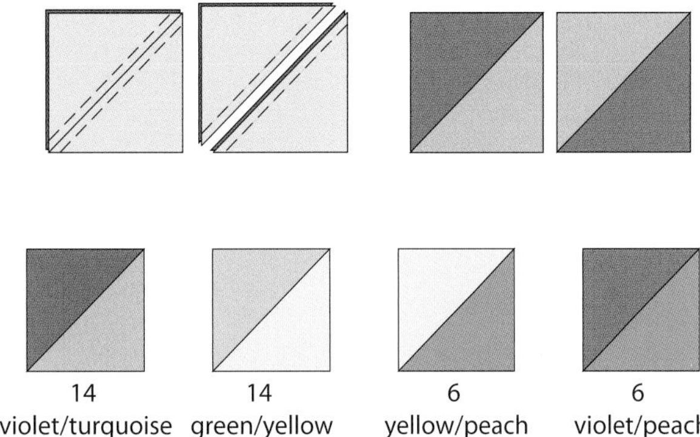

Make the Quarter-Circle Blocks

These directions are for fusing the quarter-circle blocks; for pieced quarter-circles refer to directions in the box below.

1. Following the instructions in Preparing Fused Appliqué on page 110, trace 40–5" quarter-circle curve templates onto the paper side of fusible web, marking the solid curved line and straight side lines. Cut out on the dashed lines. The 5" quarter-circle curve template is found on page 93.
2. Matching the straight side lines with the edges of $5\frac{1}{2}$" squares, fuse a quarter-circle to wrong side of the following $5\frac{1}{2}$" squares: 6 violet, 6 yellow, 10 turquoise, 10 peach, and 8 green

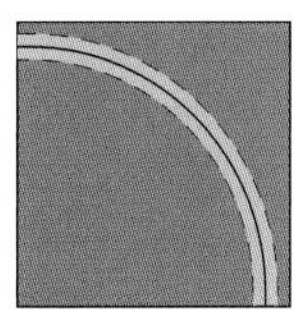

3. Cut the fabric quarter-circle on the curved solid line. Remove the paper, line up the corner of the quarter-circle with a corner of a $5\frac{1}{2}$" square and fuse in place. Stitch curve with a satin zigzag stitch, page 118, about 2mm-wide. Trim excess fabric from under quarter-circle.

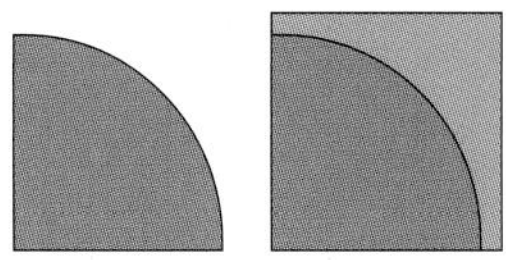

Make the following combinations.

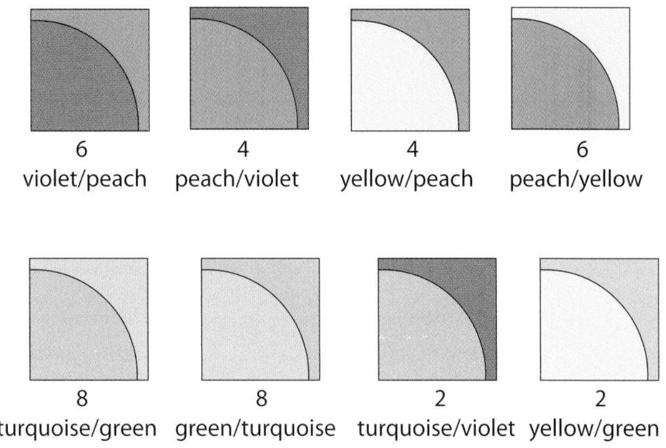

Pieced Quarter-Circle Blocks

Cut the required number of edge template A and quarter-circle template B, marking registration marks at center points of curved lines. Working with the edge piece on top, pin pieces together at center points and seam ends. Stitch, using your fingertips to keep curved edges aligned. Gently press seam toward edge piece.

Assemble the Quilt

1. Arrange the triangle-square blocks and quarter-circle blocks as shown for Quadrant A.

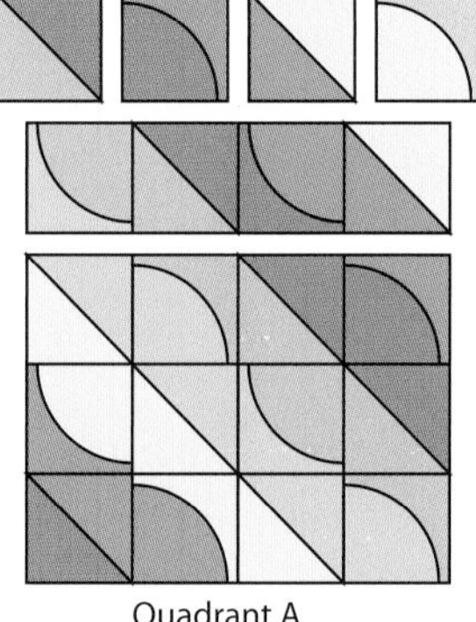

Quadrant A

2. Join blocks into rows; join rows to complete Quadrant. Make 2 Quadrant A and 2 Quadrant B.

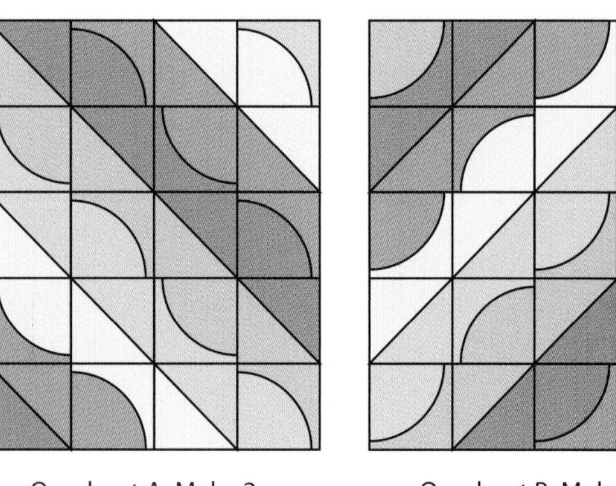

Quadrant A: Make 2 Quadrant B: Make 2

3. Rotate 1 of each Quadrant as shown below. Join Quadrants to complete quilt top.

Finish the Quilt

1. If a longarm machine is to be used for quilting, cut the backing fabric into 2–1⅜ yard lengths; join lengthwise.

2. Layer the quilt top, batting, and backing.

3. Quilt as desired. This Rainbow Twist is quilted with a feather motif.

4. Trim the excess batting and backing to straighten the edges and square the corners.

5. Stitch together the 2¼"-wide binding strips with diagonal seams to make a continuous strip. Use to bind the quilt.

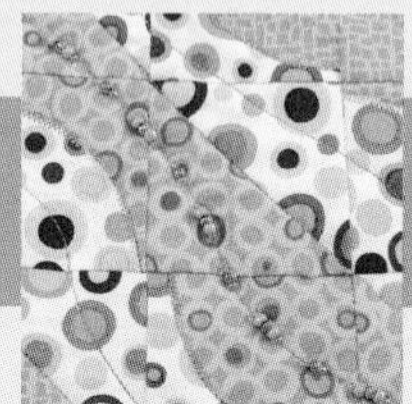

Messenger Bag

finished size: 10" x 7½"

A smaller quarter-circle pattern in a fun kid's print makes a stylish new bag to hold favorite treasures or the newest technology.

MATERIALS

Fabric

- 1 fat quarter white print for blocks
- 5/8 yard green print for blocks, bag front and strap
- 3/4 yard turquoise print for blocks, sides, and lining

Paper-Backed Fusible Web

- 1/4 yard

Quilt Batting

- 18" x 36" piece of quilt batting

- 2–7/8"-diameter rings

Fabric suggestions are 40"–42" wide.
Fat quarter = 18" x 20".

Sew all patchwork seams with a 1/4" seam allowance.

Follow manufacturer's directions for using fusible web.

Cut the Quilt Pieces

From the white print cut

- 6–3 3/8" squares
- 12–3" squares

From the green print cut

- 1–10 1/2" x 9" rectangle for bag front
- 1–3" x 22 1/2" rectangle for facing
- 1–3 1/4" x 28" strip for long strap
- 1–3 1/4" x 14" strip for short strap
- 3–3 3/8" squares
- 6–3" squares

From the turquoise print cut

- 1–12" x 26" rectangle for bag lining
- 1–10" x 12" rectangle for flap lining
- 2–1 1/2" x 7 1/2" rectangles for sides
- 2–3" x 10" rectangles for side lining
- 3–3 3/8" squares
- 6–3" squares

From the batting cut

- 1–10" x 12" rectangle for flap
- 1–12" x 26" rectangle for bag body
- 2–3" x 10" rectangles for sides

Make the Triangle-Square Blocks

1. Select 3 pairs of white/green 3 3/8" squares and 3 pairs of white/turquoise 3 3/8" squares.
2. Draw a diagonal line across wrong side of one square in each pair.
3. Stitch 1/4" from drawn line on both sides. Cut on drawn line. Press open to reveal triangle-square blocks. Press seam allowances to the darker fabric.

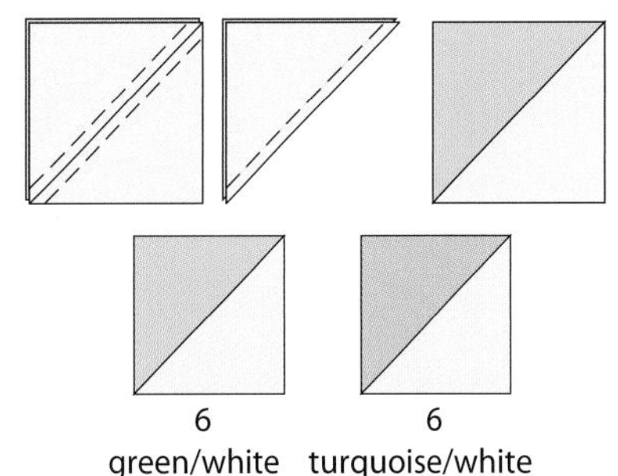

Make the Quarter-Circle Blocks

These directions are for fusing the quarter-circle blocks. If you want to piece the quarter-circles, refer to directions on page 52. Use quarter-circle template D and edge template C on page 94.

1. Following the instructions in Preparing Fused Appliqué on page 110, trace 12 quarter-circle curves onto the paper side of fusible web, marking the solid curved line and straight side lines. Cut out on the dashed lines. The 2½" quarter-circle curve template is found on page 94.
2. Matching the straight side lines with the edges of 3" squares, fuse a quarter-circle to wrong side of the following 3" squares: 6 white, 3 green, and 3 turquoise.

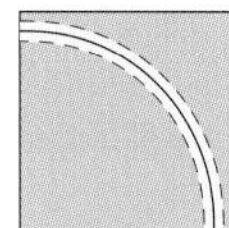

3. Cut the fabric quarter-circle on the curved solid line. Remove the paper, line up the corner of the quarter-circle with a corner of 3" square and fuse in place. Stitch curve with a satin zigzag stitch, page 118, about 2mm-wide. Trim excess fabric from under quarter-circle.

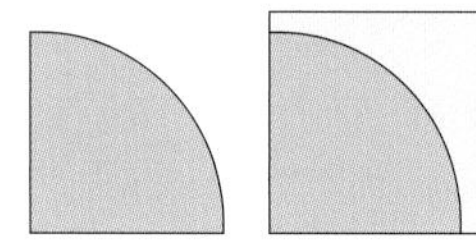

Make the following combinations.

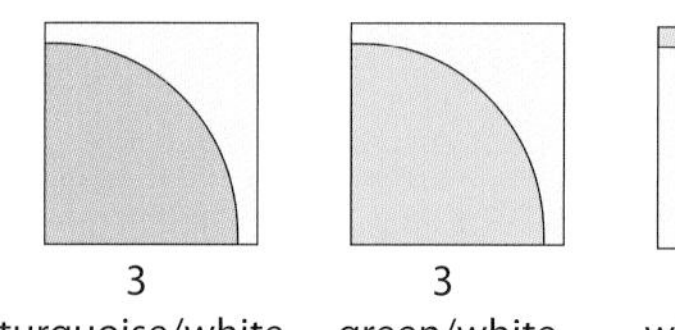

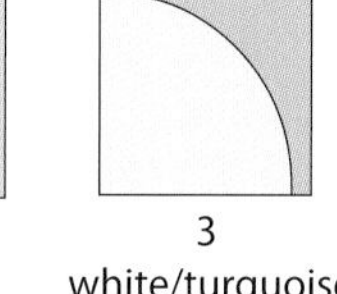

3	3	3	3
turquoise/white	green/white	white/green	white/turquoise

Assemble the Front Flap and Bag Back

1. Arrange the triangle-square blocks and quarter-circle blocks.
2. Join blocks into rows; join rows to make Front Flap and Bag Back.

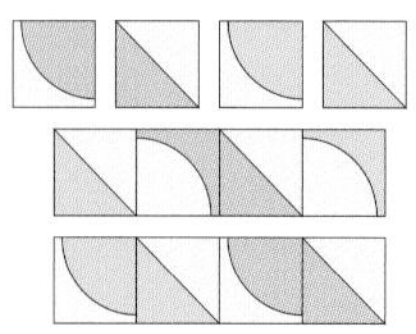

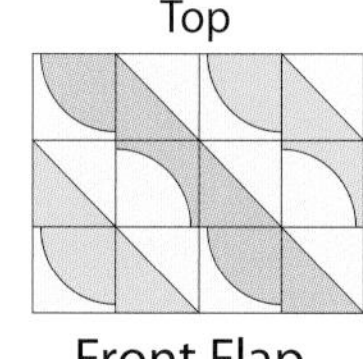

Top

Front Flap

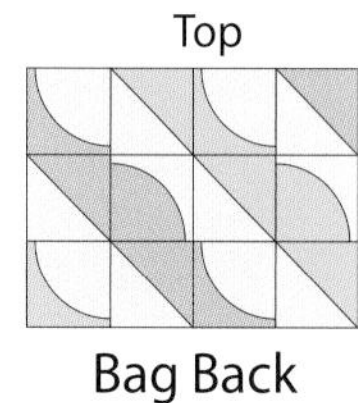

Top

Bag Back

Assemble Front Flap

1. Layer front flap batting rectangle, pieced Front Flap (right side up) and flap lining (right side down). Stitch around the 2 sides and the bottom, gently rounding corners. Leave top of flap open for turning. Trim the excess batting and lining to straighten the edges; trim corner curves.
2. Turn right side out.
3. Quilt in the ditch and in a wave through center of each color. Top stitch close to turned edge.

Assemble Bag Body

1. Stitch Bag Back to Bag Front.

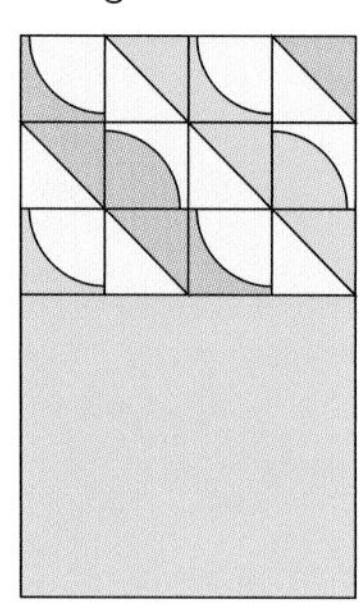

Bag Back & Front

2. Layer bag lining rectangle, bag batting rectangle, and Bag Back/Front.
3. Quilt similar to Front Flap.
4. Trim the excess batting and lining to straighten the edges and square the corners.
5. Layer 1 side lining, 1 side batting, and 1 side rectangle. Quilt as desired. Trim quilted side to measure 1½" x 8". Make 2 quilted sides.
6. Stitch quilted side to front and back of bag, right sides together and aligning top edges. Start stitching at top and stop ¼" from bottom of side; backstitch to secure stitching.

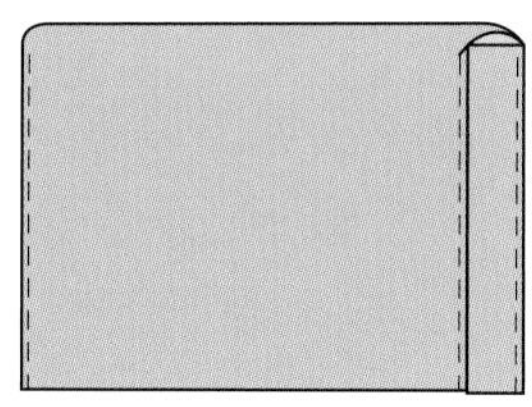

7. Clip seam allowance of bag almost to stitching at each corner.
8. Align bottom of bag with bottom edge of side. Stitch seam, backstitching at each end.

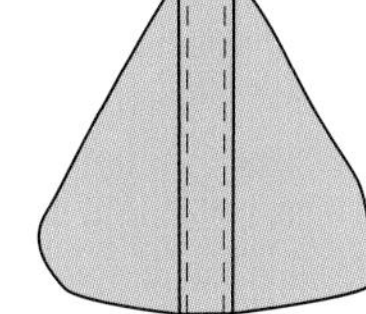

9. Repeat for other side.

10. Zigzag or overcast the seams.

11. Turn the bag right side out.

Finish the Bag

1. With right sides facing, baste quilted flap to bag back at top edge.

2. Join ends of facing rectangle to form a continuous strip. Press 1/2" of one long edge of strip to the wrong side. Stitch close to edge to hem facing.

3. With right sides together, pin the raw edge of facing to the top of bag.

4. Stitch through all layers around top of bag, encasing flap.

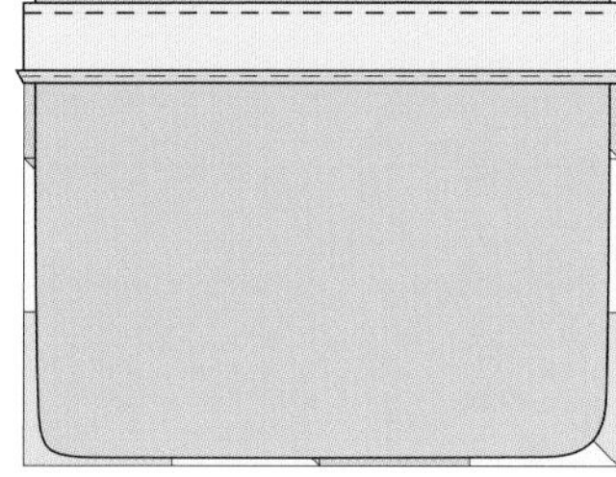

5. Press seam toward facing. Top stitch about 1/8" from the seam through facing and seam allowance only.

6. Press facing to the inside of bag. Hand stitch facing to lining.

Straps

1. Press 1 strap in half lengthwise with wrong sides together to create center fold.

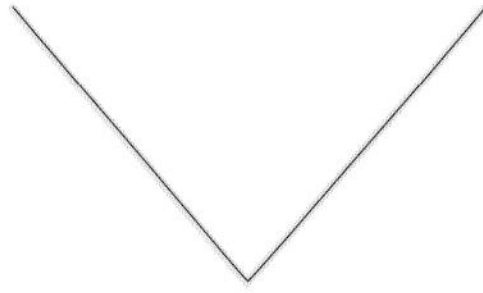

2. Open strap and press both edges so they meet at the center fold.

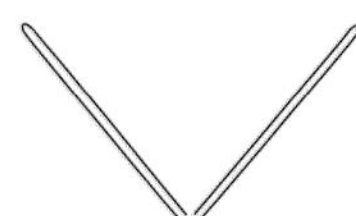

3. Repress strap in half, concealing raw edges in fold. Machine topstitch along both edges of strap. Make 2 straps.

4. Turn under 1/2" on end of short strap. Topstitch to left side of bag positioning about 2" from top edge. Stitch a square and then an X as shown to secure the strap. Repeat with long strap to right side of bag.

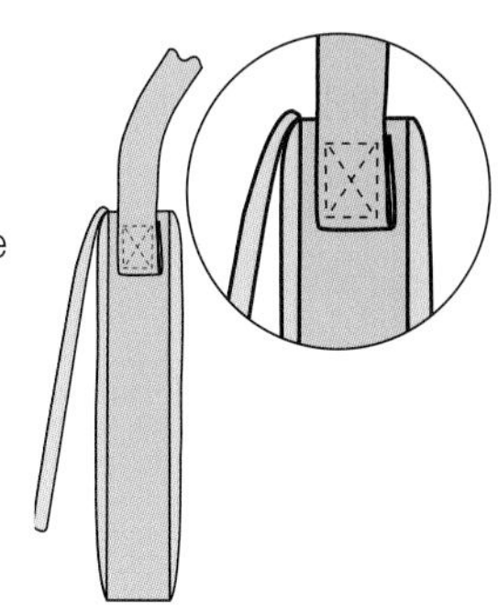

5. Place rings at loose end of long strap. Fold up 1 1/4", turn under 1/4" and stitch in place.

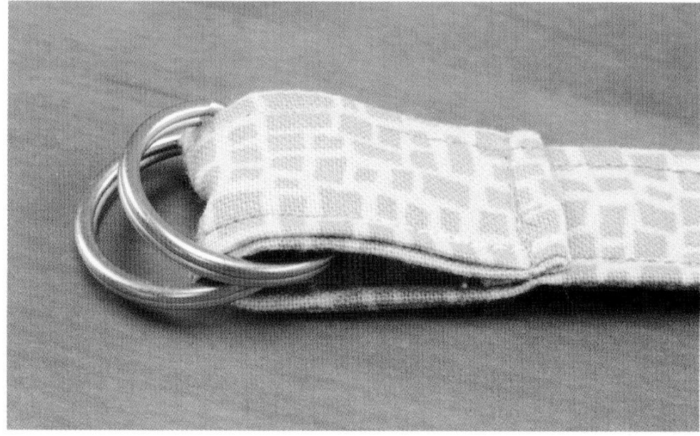

6. Hem loose end of short strap. Thread hemmed end through rings. Adjust strap to desired length.

7. If desired, embellish the bag with beads referring to Beading on page 122.

Rainbow Twist

Ideas for Making Larger Quilts

Rainbow Twist
6 Quadrant - 50" x 60"

Rainbow Twist
8 Quadrant - 50" x 80"

Rainbow Twist can easily be made into a larger quilt. Construct 3 or 4 of Quadrant A and B. Follow the illustrations for setting options for a 50" x 60" and a 50" x 80" quilt. Add borders to make the quilt even larger.

Decorative Stitching

There is a wonderful variety of threads available for stitching appliqué. You will want to experiment to see which threads you prefer. For Rainbow Twist I chose size 30-weight variegated thread. When stitching fabrics like the batiks used in Rainbow Twist, a variegated thread blends with the colors.

Rainbow Twist

Ideas for Other Color Schemes

Analogous Color Scheme

Choose an analogous color scheme. All colors in an analogous color scheme have a primary color in common. The illustration shown has the primary color green in common.

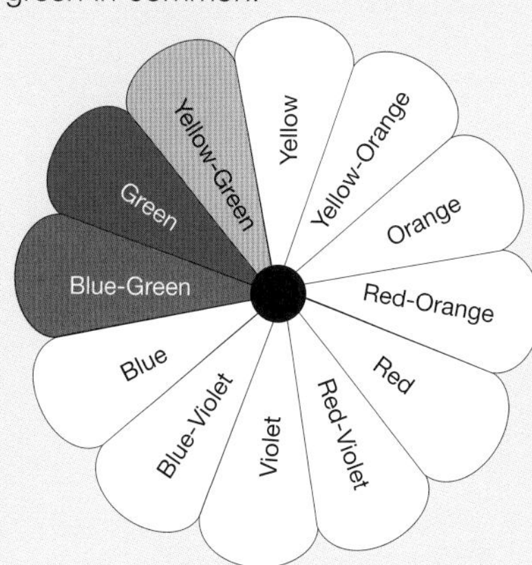

Two Color Scheme

Choose a two color scheme with a high contrast in color and value. Above, I chose a kid-friendly fish print as the darker value and a coordinating gold as the contrasting value. At right, is a four-quadrant two color scheme.

Using the Color Wheel

Playing with the colors in Rainbow Twist is a good time to talk with younger children about the colors of a rainbow. For older kids, talk about the color wheel and how colors are mixed. Refer to Getting Kids Involved on page 5.

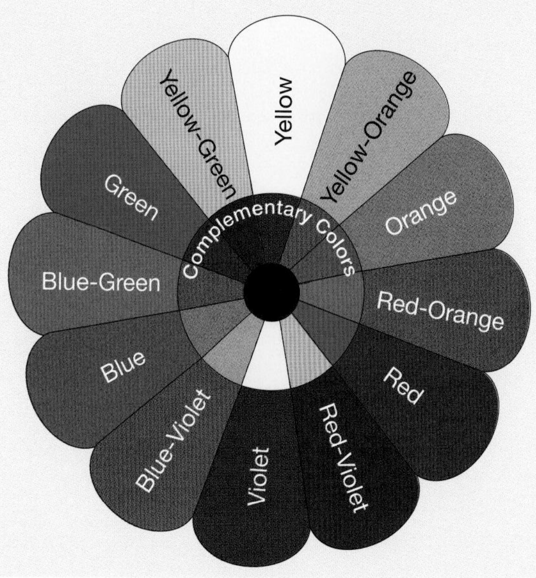

Zany Zoo

finished size 44" x 57"

Make fanciful zoo characters—
a Unicorn, a Tiger, and a Lion—come alive in a wonky setting.

MATERIALS

Blocks, Borders, and Binding

- 1 fat quarter white print for blocks
- 1 3/8 yards brown dot print #1 for blocks and binding
- 1 yard each of 2 different brown dot print for blocks
- 1/4 yard (or 1 fat quarter) green print for blocks
- 1/4 yard (or 1 fat quarter) pink print for blocks
- 1/4 yard (or 1 fat quarter) gold print for blocks
- 1/4 yard (or 1 fat quarter) turquoise print for blocks
- 3/4 yard blue print for blocks and outer border
- 1/2 yard purple print for blocks and inner border

Appliqué

- Fat quarters or smaller assorted prints in green, turquoise, orange, blue, violet, pink, and gold for animal blocks

Backing

- 3 yards backing fabric

Paper-Backed Fusible Web

- 1 yard

Quilt Batting

- 50" x 63" piece of quilt batting (or Twin-size batting)

- 12 1/2" square ruler or 12 1/2" square template plastic
- 6 1/2" square ruler or 6 1/2" square template plastic

Fabric suggestions are 40"–42" wide. Fat quarter = 18" x 20".

Sew all patchwork seams with a 1/4" seam allowance.

Follow manufacturer's directions for using fusible web.

Cut the Quilt Pieces

From the white print cut

- 3–8" squares for animal block centers

From brown dot print #1 cut

- 6–2 1/4"-wide strips for binding
- 2–3 1/2" x 16" rectangles for animal blocks
- 2–3 1/2" x 10" rectangles for animal blocks
- 24–2 1/2" x 9" rectangles for wonky blocks
- 24–2 1/2" x 5" rectangles for wonky blocks

From each remaining brown dot print cut

- 2–3 1/2" x 16" rectangles for animal blocks
- 2–3 1/2" x 10" rectangles for animal blocks
- 24–2 1/2" x 9" rectangles for wonky blocks
- 24–2 1/2" x 5" rectangles for wonky blocks

From green print cut

- 2–1 1/2" x 10" rectangles for animal block inner borders
- 2–1 1/2" x 8" rectangles for animal block inner borders
- 6–5" squares for wonky block centers

From pink print cut

- 2–1 1/2" x 10" rectangles for animal block inner borders
- 2–1 1/2" x 8" rectangles for animal block inner borders
- 6–5" squares for wonky block centers

From gold print cut

- 6–5" squares for wonky block centers

From turquoise print cut

- 2–1 1/2" x 10" rectangles for animal block inner borders
- 2–1 1/2" x 8" rectangles for animal block inner borders
- 6–5" squares for wonky block centers

From blue print cut

- 6–5" squares for wonky block centers
- 3–3 1/2"-wide strips. Join strips, then cut 2–3 1/2" x 57 1/2" outer side borders.
- 2–3 1/2" x 38 1/2" inner top and bottom borders

From purple print cut

- 6–5" squares for wonky block centers
- 3–1 1/2"-wide strips. Join strips, then cut 2–1 1/2" x 51 1/2" inner side borders.
- 3–1 1/2" x 36 1/2" inner horizontal borders

Zany Animal Blocks

1. Lay out 1 white square, 1 set of matching 1½"-wide rectangles, and 1 set of matching brown dot 3½"-wide rectangles as shown. Join to complete 1 animal block background. Make 3 animal block backgrounds.

Prepare the Appliqué Pieces

Following the instructions in Preparing Fused Appliqué on page 110, build the following animal units on non-stick pressing sheets or parchment paper. The patterns are found on pages 95-102, the layouts on page 103. Make a Unicorn, Tiger, and Lion as shown, or choose your 3 favorite zoo animals from the animal patterns.

Note: The layouts can be enlarged and used to arrange appliqué pieces and mark detail lines.

Unicorn

- 1–Unicorn Muzzle
- 1–Unicorn Head
- 1 set–Unicorn Horn A - E
- 1–Unicorn Left Ear and Left Ear Top
- 1–Unicorn Right Ear and Right Ear Top
- 1–Unicorn Bangs
- 2–Unicorn Mane
- 1 set Nostrils
- 2–Eyeball
- 2–Eye Pupil

Tiger

- 1–Tiger Head
- 1–Tiger Left Outer Ear and Left Inner Ear
- 1–Tiger Right Outer Ear and Right Inner Ear
- 1 set–Tiger Stripes
- 1–Tiger Nose
- 2–Eyeball
- 2–Eye Pupil

Lion

- 1–Lion Head
- 1–Lion Left Outer Ear and Left Inner Ear
- 1–Lion Right Outer Ear and Right Inner Ear
- 16–Lion Mane
- 1–Lion Nose
- 1–Lion Nose Bridge
- 2–Eyeball
- 2–Eye Pupil

Stitch the Appliqué

1. Position 1 set of animal appliqué pieces on 1 pieced animal block background. Fuse in place.
2. Stitch the appliqué with a satin zigzag stitch, page 118, using matching or contrasting thread.
3. Add details to animal faces, referring to Stitching Mouths and Lines on page 121.

Trim the Blocks

1. Trim animal blocks to tilted 12½" square as shown, using a 12½" square ruler. Make sure edge of ruler is at least ½" away from every inner border corner.

2. Tilt 2 animal blocks to the right and tilt 1 animal block to the left.

Blocks Tilted Right
Cut 2

Block Tilted Left
Cut 1

Note: If not using a 12½" square ruler, place 12½" square template plastic on animal block. Draw around square. Cut on drawn line.

Wonky Blocks

1. Lay out print 5" square and 1 set of matching brown dot 2½"-wide rectangles as shown. Join to make 1 block. Make 36 blocks; 6 of each center color.)

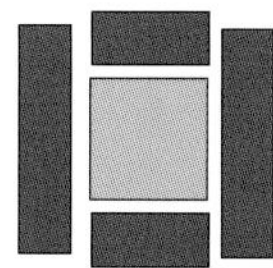
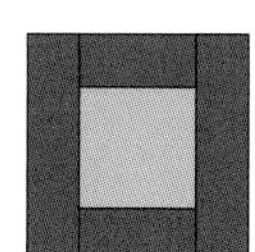

2. To make blocks wonky, trim to 6½" square as shown, using a 6½" square ruler. Make sure edge of ruler is at least ½" away from every center square corner. Tilt 3 squares of each color to the right and tilt 3 squares of each color to the left.

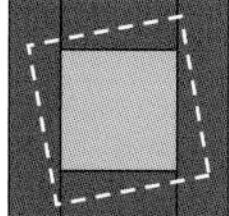
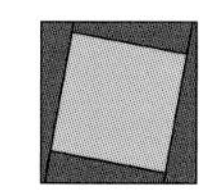

Square Tilted Right

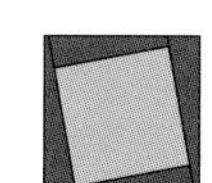

Square Tilted Left

Note: If not using a 6½" square ruler, place 6½" square template plastic on animal block. Draw around square. Cut on drawn line.

Assemble the Quilt

1. Arrange the animal blocks, wonky blocks, and purple inner horizontal borders. Join into rows; join rows to complete quilt center.

2. Sew the purple inner side borders to the quilt center.

3. Sew the blue outer top and bottom borders to the quilt center. Sew the blue outer side borders to the quilt.

Finish the Quilt

1. Cut the backing fabric into 2–1½ yard lengths; join lengthwise.

2. Layer the quilt top, batting, and backing.

3. Refer to Quilting Appliqué on page 126 and quilt as desired.

4. Trim the excess batting and backing to straighten the edges and square the corners.

5. Stitch together the brown 2¼"-wide strips with diagonal seams to make a continuous strip. Use to bind the quilt.

Zany Zoo Pillow Sham

finished size: 26" x 20"

Just for fun, make a matching pillow sham for the Zany Zoo Quilt using another zany zoo animal block.

MATERIALS

Appliqué

- Assorted fabrics for appliqué

Block Background

- 1/4 yard (or 1 fat quarter) white print

Borders and Pillow Back

- 1/4 yard (or 1 fat quarter) violet print
- 1/4 yard (or 1 fat quarter) brown and green dot
- 1/4 yard (or 1 fat quarter) green print
- 1/4 yard brown and turquoise dot
- 1 1/4 yards turquoise print

Lining

- 24" x 30" piece of muslin

Paper-Backed Fusible Web

- 1/2 yard

Quilt Batting

- 24" x 30" piece of quilt batting

- Standard bed pillow

- 12 1/2" square ruler or 12 1/2" square template plastic

Fabric suggestions are 40"–42" wide.
Fat quarter = 18" x 20".

Sew all patchwork seams with a 1/4" seam allowance.

Follow manufacturer's directions for using fusible web.

Cut the Pillow Pieces

From the white print cut

- 1–8" square for animal block center

From violet print cut

- 2–1 1/2" x 10" rectangles for animal block inner borders
- 2–1 1/2" x 8" rectangles for animal block inner borders

From brown and green dot cut

- 2–3 1/2" x 16" rectangles for animal block
- 2–3 1/2" x 10" rectangles for animal block

From green print cut

- 2–2" x 15 1/2" rectangles for inner border
- 2–2" x 12 1/2" rectangles for inner border

From brown and turquoise dot cut

- 2–3" x 20 1/2" rectangles for middle border
- 2–3" x 15 1/2" rectangles for middle border

From turquoise print cut

- 2–3 1/2" x 20 1/2" strips for outer side borders
- 2–20 1/2" x 32 1/2" back rectangles

Animal Block

1. Lay out white square, violet 1 1/2"-wide rectangles, and brown and green dot 3 1/2"-wide rectangles as shown. Join to complete animal block background.

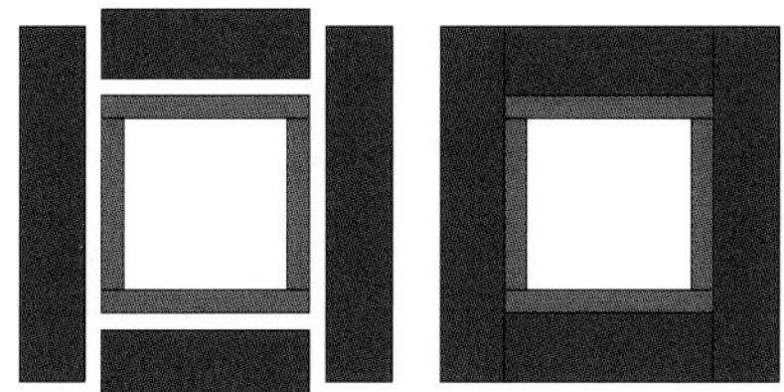

Prepare the Appliqué Pieces

Following the instructions in Preparing Fused Appliqué on page 110, build the animal unit of your choice on non-stick pressing sheet or parchment paper. The patterns are found on pages 95-102, and the layouts on page 103.

Stitch the Appliqué

1. Position the animal unit on block background. Fuse in place.

2. Stitch the appliqué with a satin zigzag stitch, page 118, using matching or contrasting thread.

3. Add details to animal face, referring to Stitching Mouths and Lines on page 121.

Trim the Block

Trim animal block to a right tilted 12½" square as shown, using a12½" square ruler. Make sure edge of ruler is at least ½" away from every inner border corner.

Note: If not using a 12½" square ruler, place 12½" square template plastic on animal block. Draw around square. Cut on drawn line.

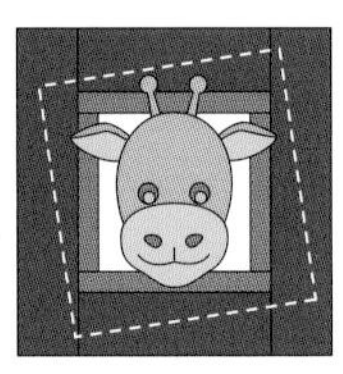

Assemble the Pillow Top

1. Lay out animal block, green 2"-wide borders, brown and turquoise dot 2½"-wide borders, and turquoise 3½"-wide borders as shown. Join to complete pillow top.

2. Layer the pillow top, batting, and lining.

3. Refer to Quilting Appliqué on page 126 and quilt as desired.

4. Trim the excess batting and lining to straighten the edges and square the corners.

Finish the Pillow Sham

1. Fold each back rectangle in half with wrong sides facing.

2. Lay the back rectangles together overlapping the folded edges to make a 26½" x 20½" rectangle.

3. Baste across the overlap to hold while joining to pillow top.

4. With right sides together lay the pillow top on the pillow back. Trim the back to the size of the front. The quilting may have made the top shrink slightly.

5. Sew around all four sides with ¼" seam allowance making rounded corners, page 17. Trim the corners to a scant ¼" from the stitching line.

6. Turn right side out.

7. Insert bed pillow.

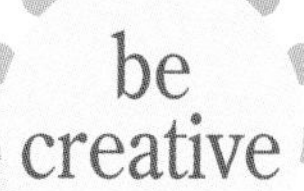

Zany Zoo

Want to try some other zany animals? Find all the zany animals and layouts on pages 95-103.

Zoo Babies

For this wallhanging make six of the animal block backgrounds, appliqué a zany animal to each and trim with three tilting left and three tilting right. Stitch together and add side, top, and bottom borders. For more fun make the bottom border wider and add the letters ZANY ZOO or your child's name.

Wonky Alphabet

The patchwork bottom of the Zany Zoo quilt is covered with wonky blocks with centers the same size as the alphabet puzzle blocks. Add letters to the blocks to make a Wonky Alphabet quilt.

Tip: For zebra head cut four 6" square pieces of stripe fabric on the true 45-degree bias. Sew together to form a chevron. Cut from the head pattern positioning the seams as indicated on the pattern.

Trim a Pillowcase

For a pillowcase coordinated to any of the quilts in this book, add a 1" fused strip of fabric around a purchased pillowcase where the hem is turned up.

Puzzle Tab

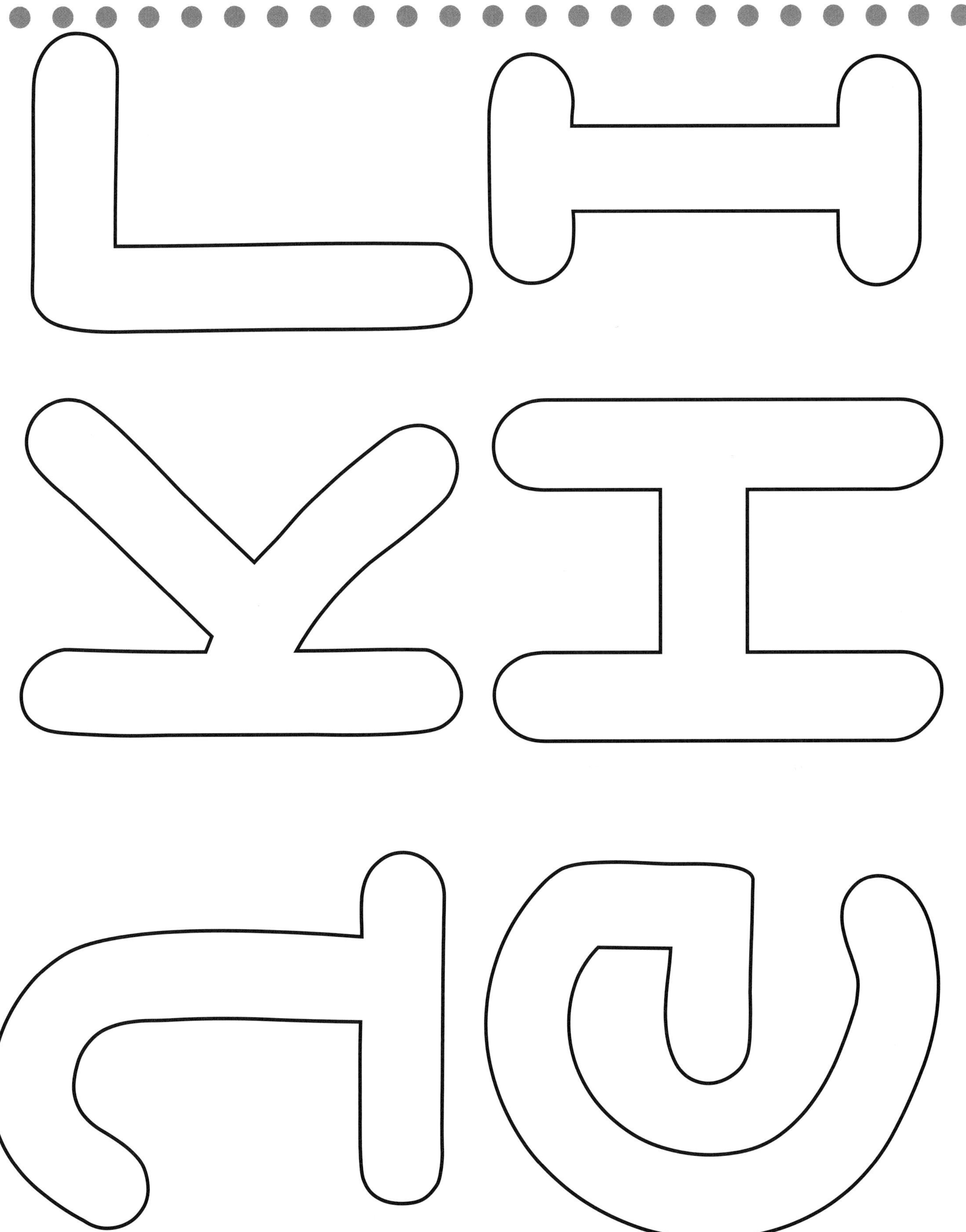

Cut 1 for M and 1 for W

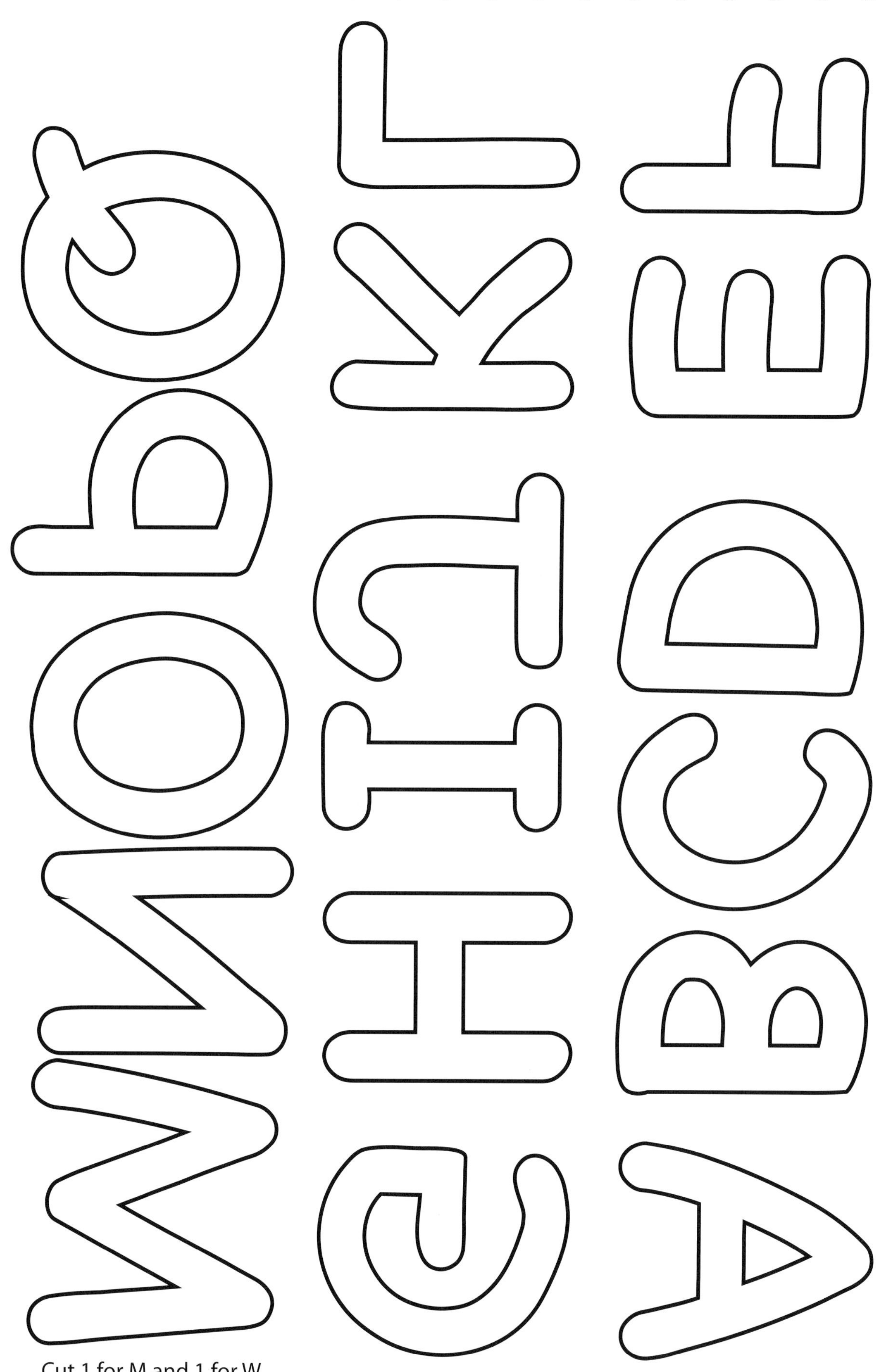

Cut 1 for M and 1 for W

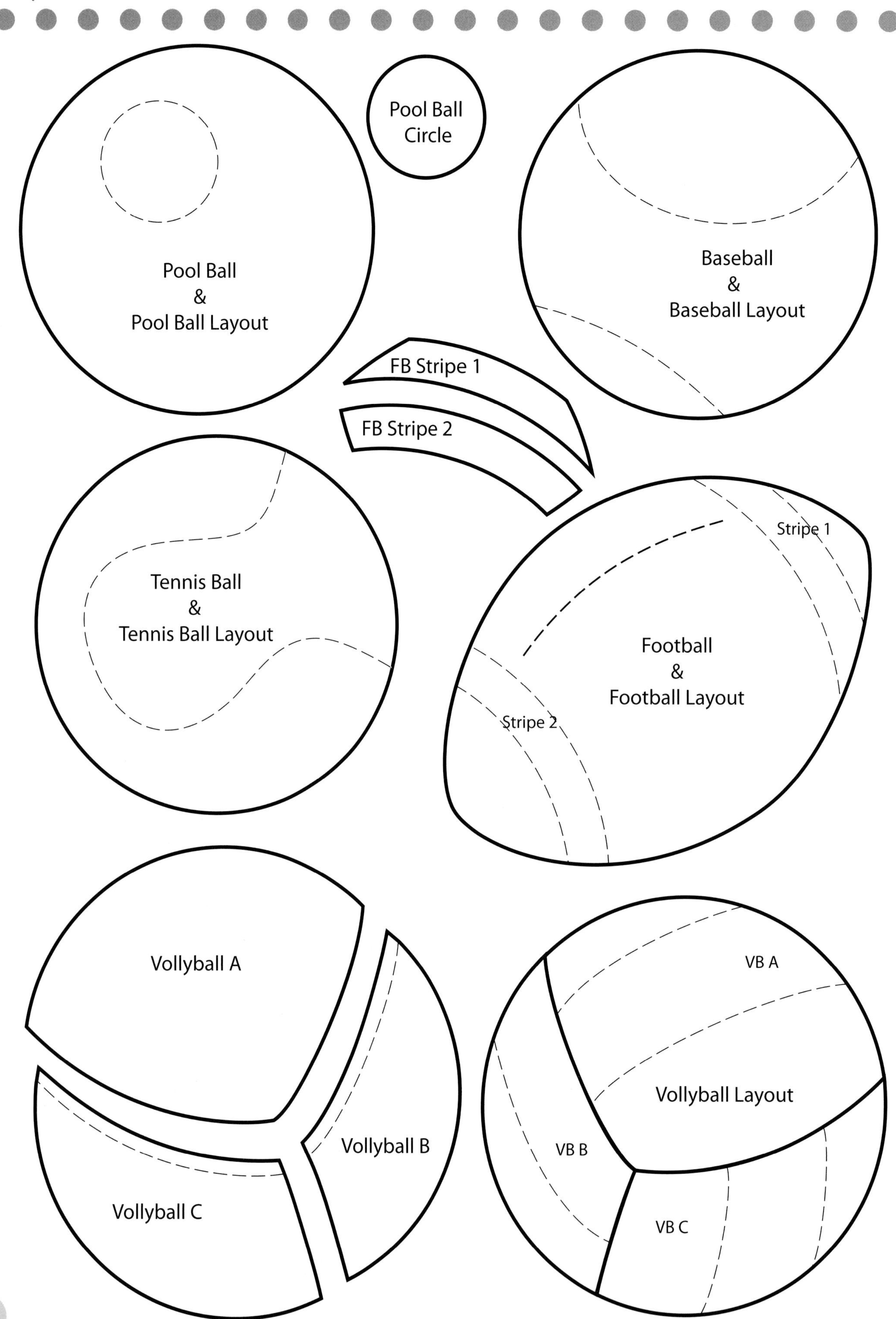
Pool Ball Circle
Pool Ball & Pool Ball Layout
Baseball & Baseball Layout
FB Stripe 1
FB Stripe 2
Tennis Ball & Tennis Ball Layout
Stripe 1
Stripe 2
Football & Football Layout
Vollyball A
Vollyball B
Vollyball C
VB A
VB B
VB C
Vollyball Layout

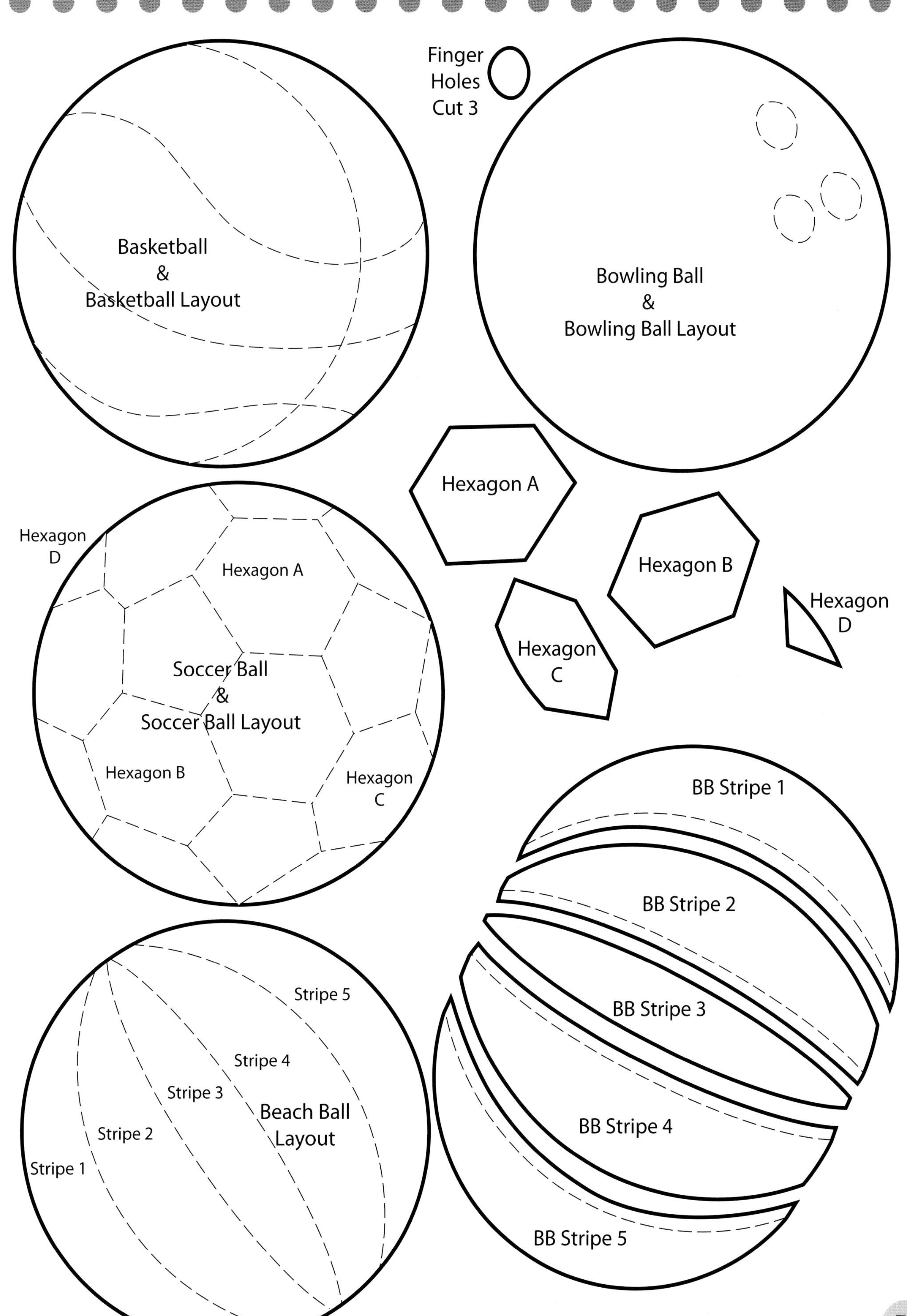
Finger
Holes
Cut 3
Basketball
&
Basketball Layout
Bowling Ball
&
Bowling Ball Layout
Hexagon A
Hexagon B
Hexagon C
Hexagon D
Hexagon D
Hexagon A
Soccer Ball
&
Soccer Ball Layout
Hexagon B
Hexagon C
BB Stripe 1
BB Stripe 2
BB Stripe 3
BB Stripe 4
BB Stripe 5
Stripe 5
Stripe 4
Stripe 3
Beach Ball
Layout
Stripe 2
Stripe 1

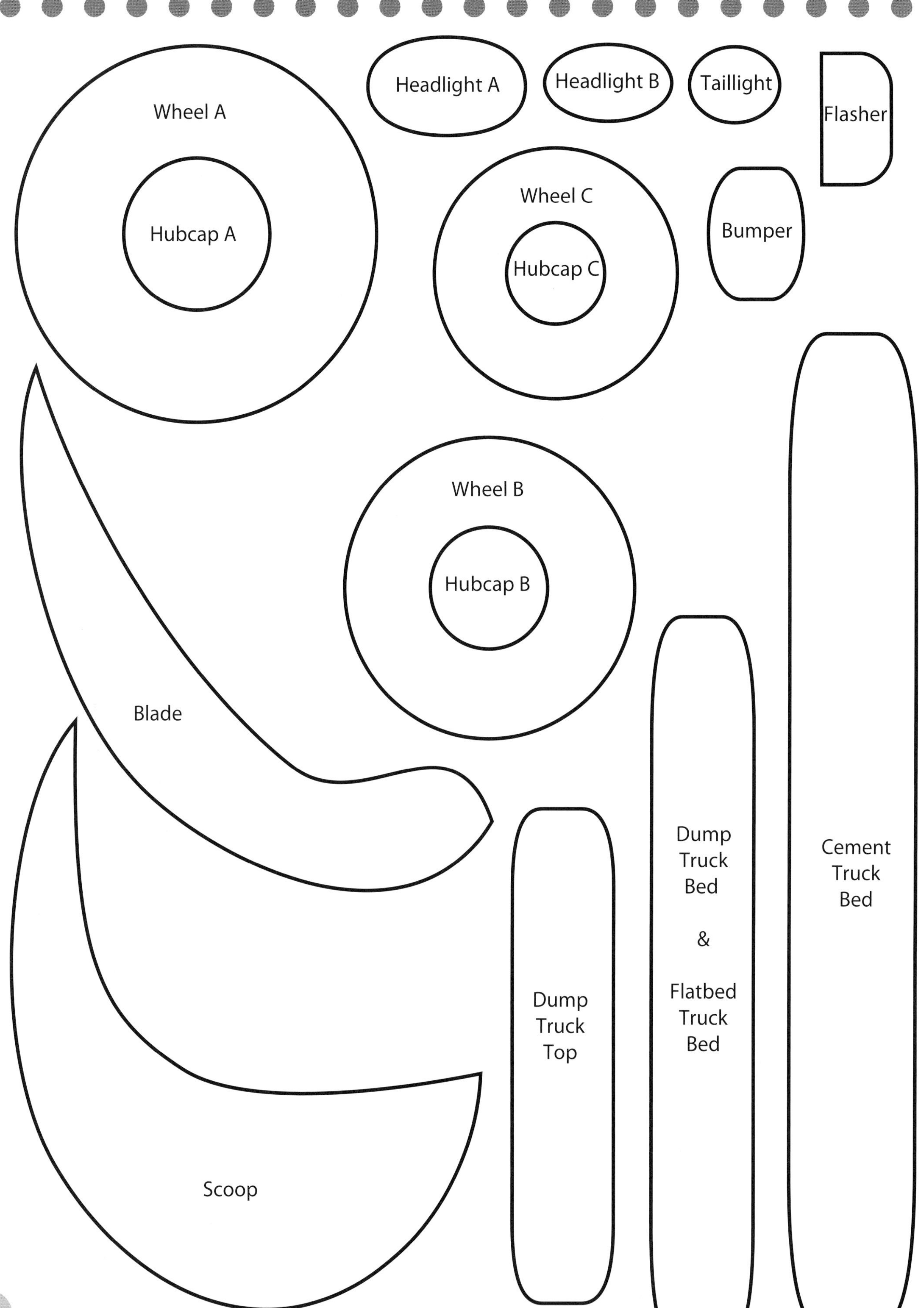
Headlight A
Headlight B
Taillight
Flasher
Wheel A
Hubcap A
Wheel C
Hubcap C
Bumper
Wheel B
Hubcap B
Blade
Dump Truck Bed & Flatbed Truck Bed
Cement Truck Bed
Dump Truck Top
Scoop

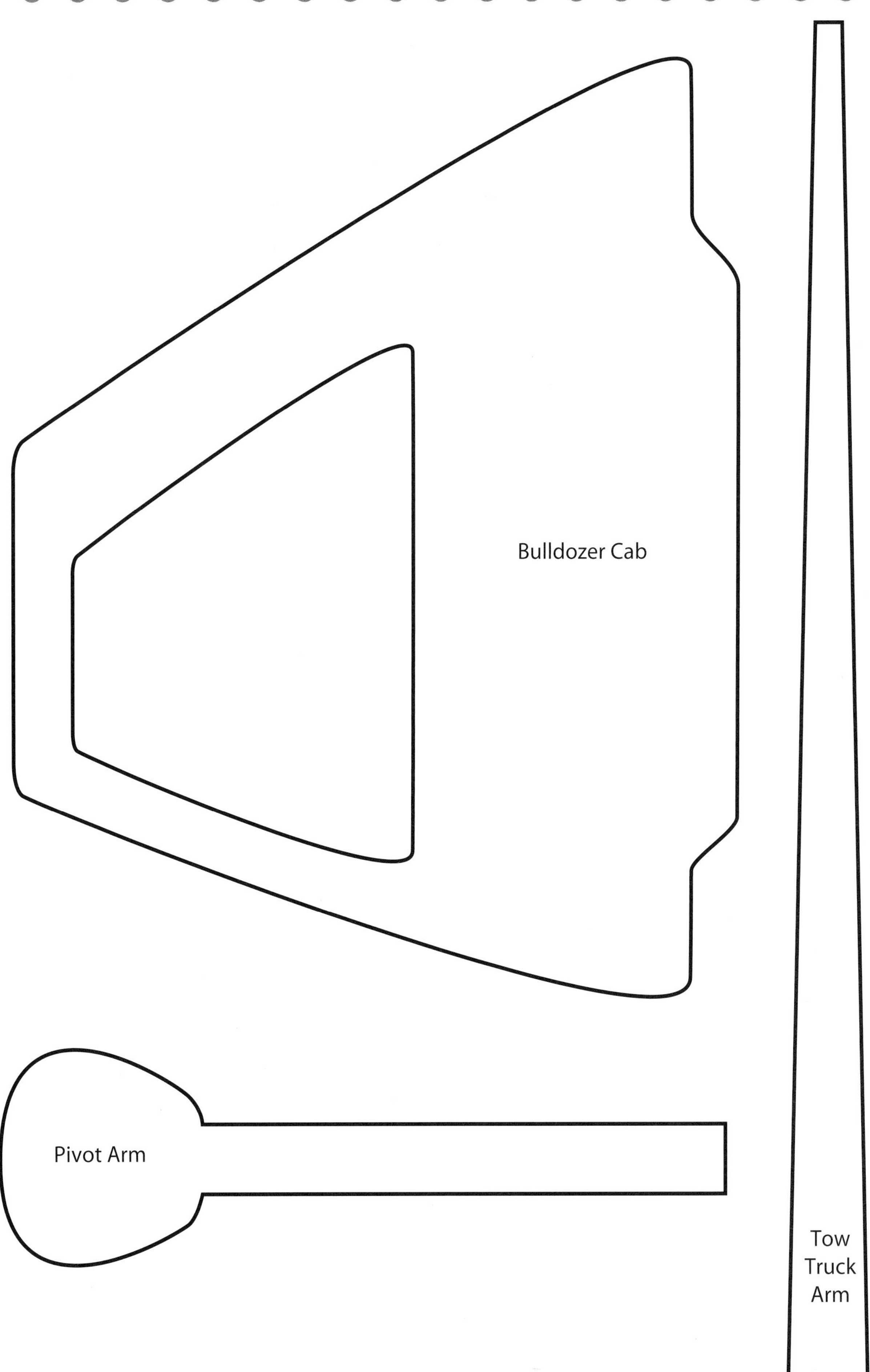
Bulldozer Cab
Pivot Arm
Tow
Truck
Arm

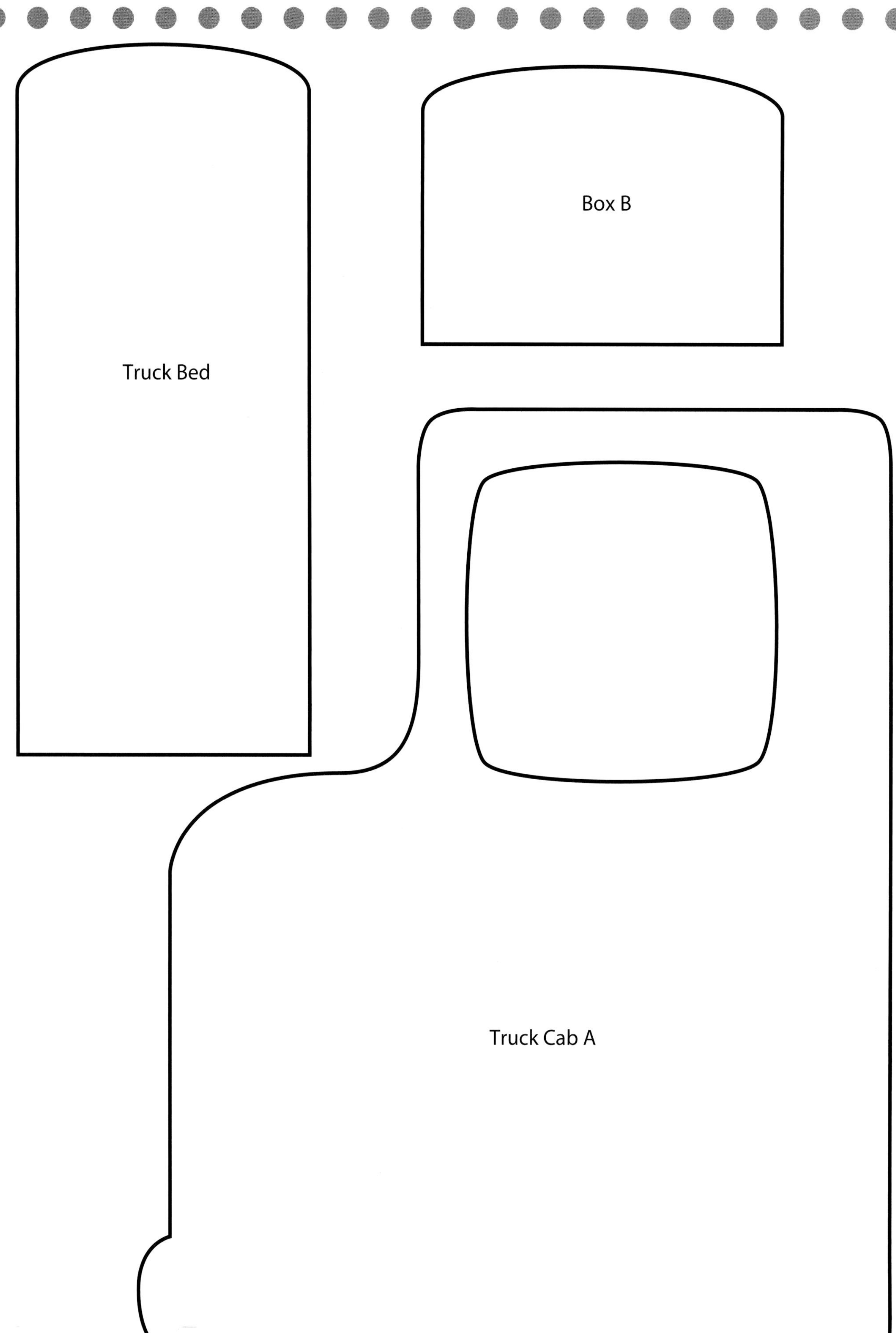
Truck Bed
Box B
Truck Cab A

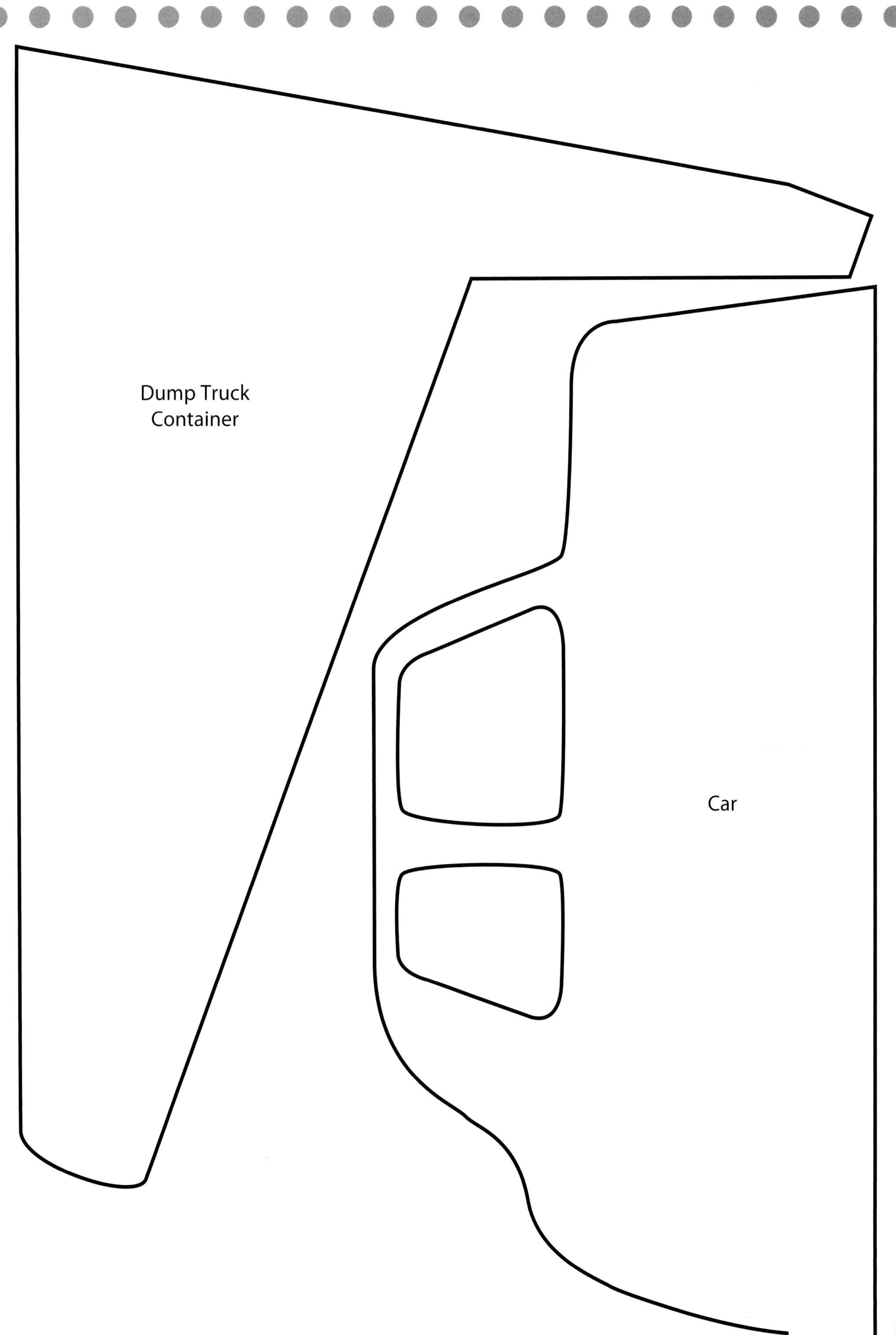
Dump Truck
Container
Car

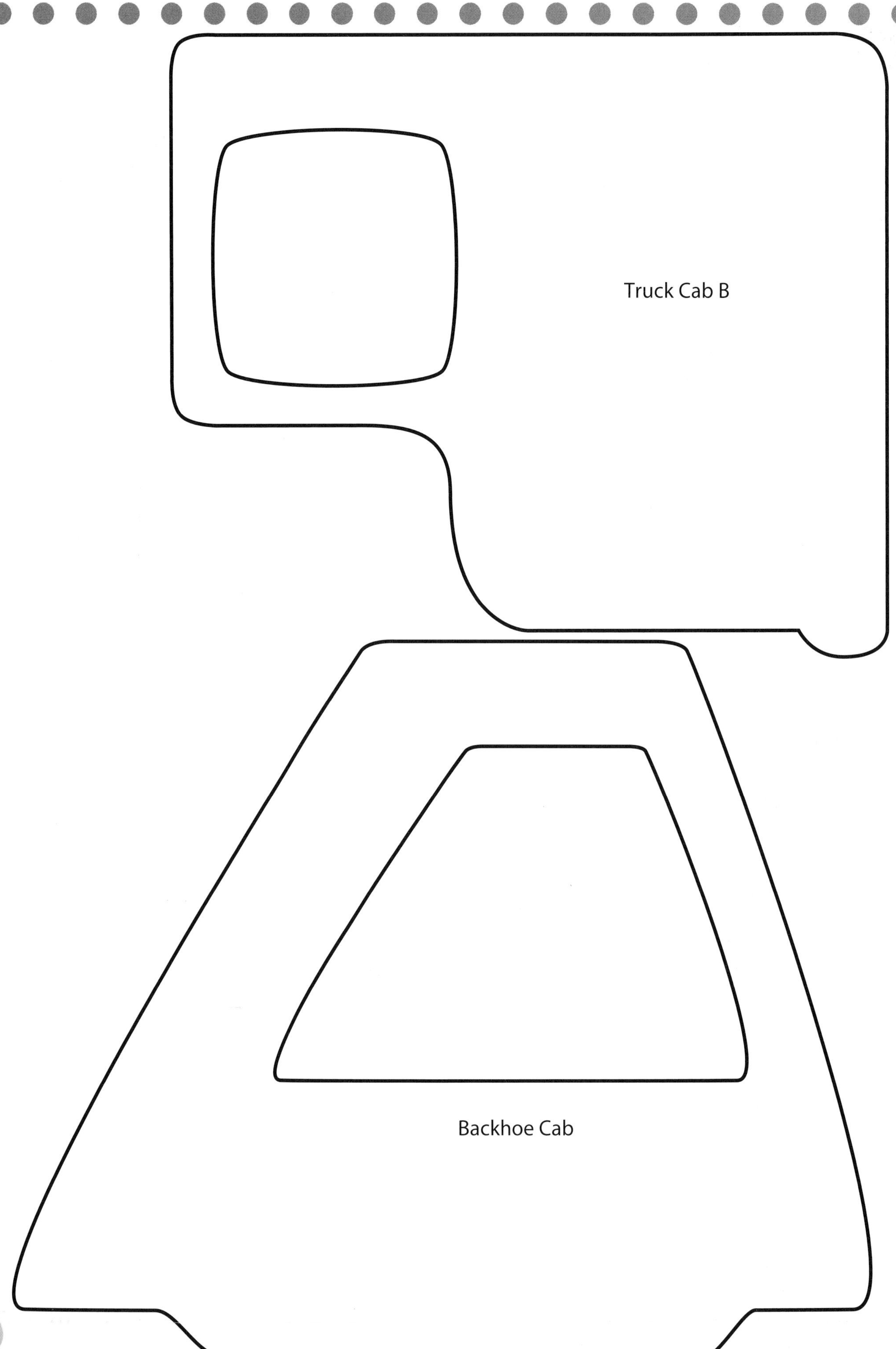
Truck Cab B
Backhoe Cab

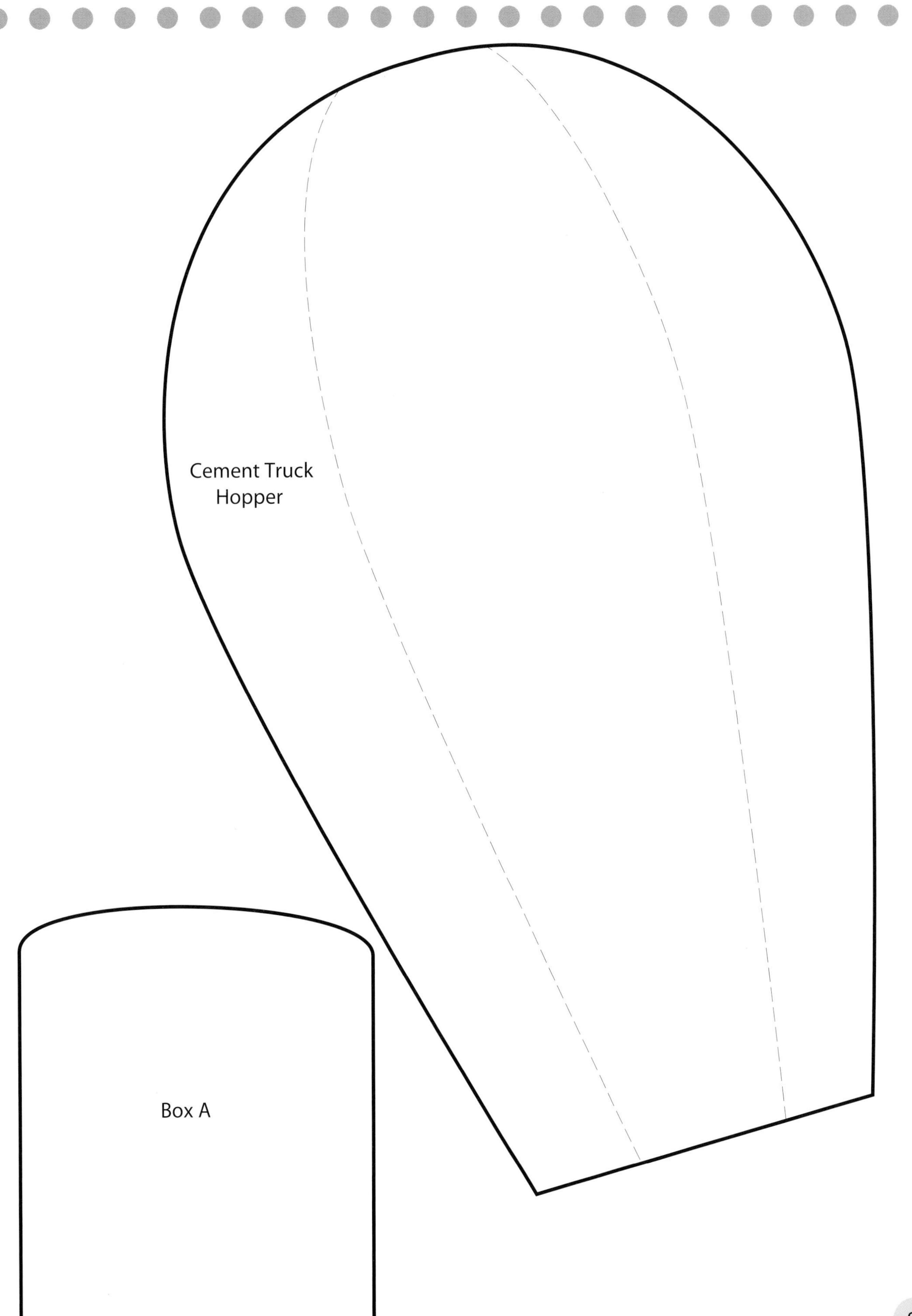
Cement Truck
Hopper
Box A

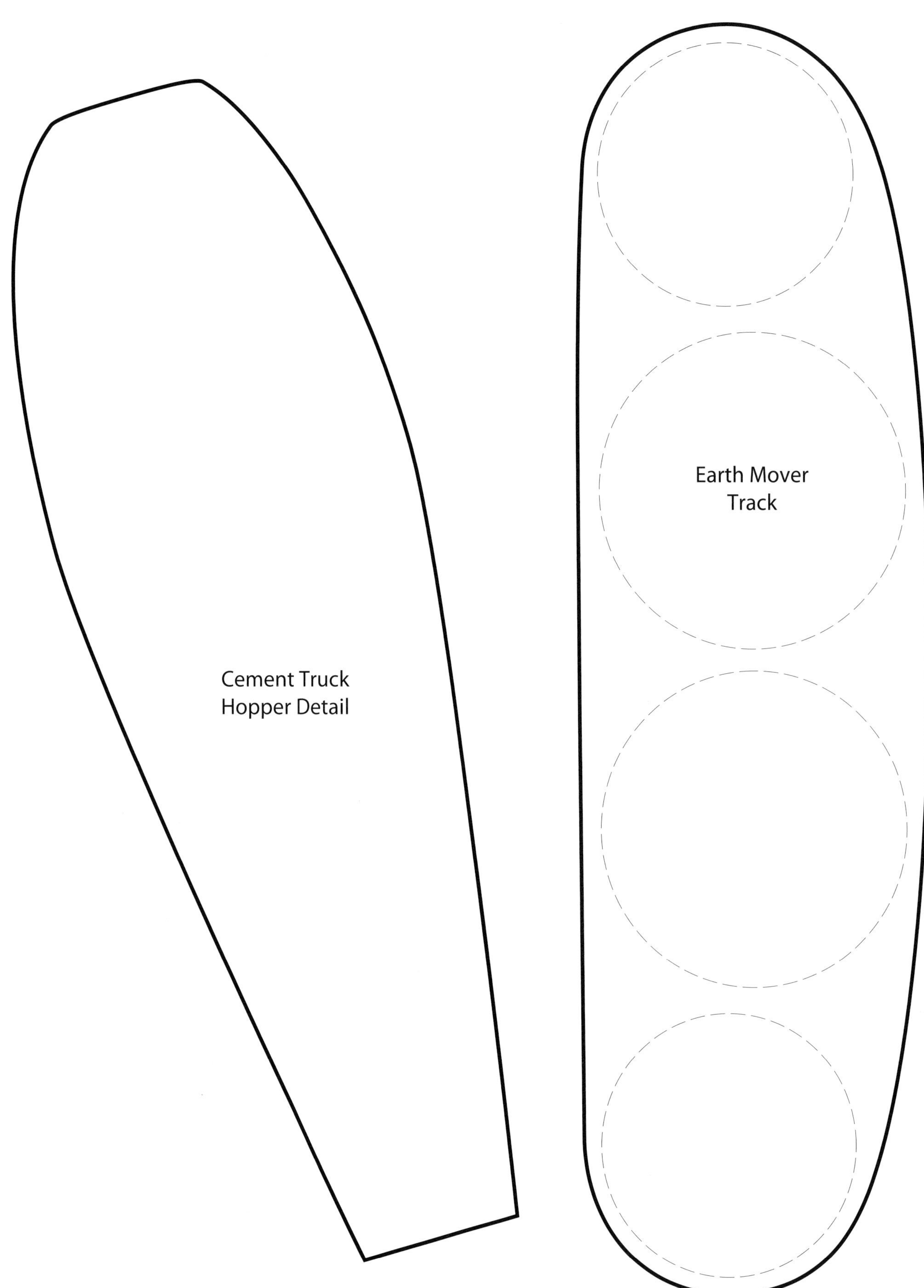
Cement Truck
Hopper Detail
Earth Mover
Track

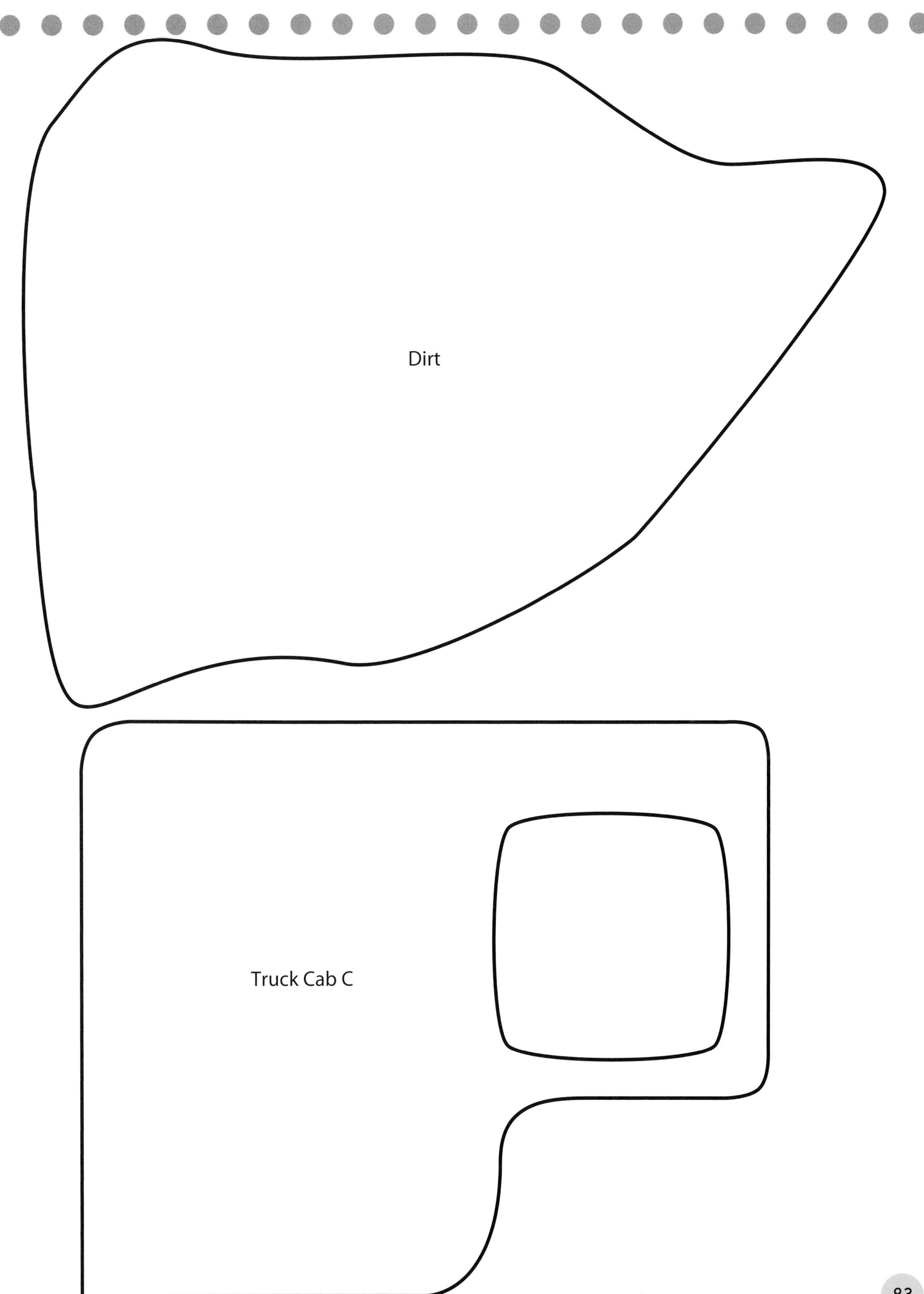
Dirt
Truck Cab C

Use these layouts as guides for pattern placement to build a motif. For full-size layouts copy at 400%, keeping in mind that many of these layouts are larger than a standard sheet of paper. To download full-size layouts go to www.landauerpub.com.

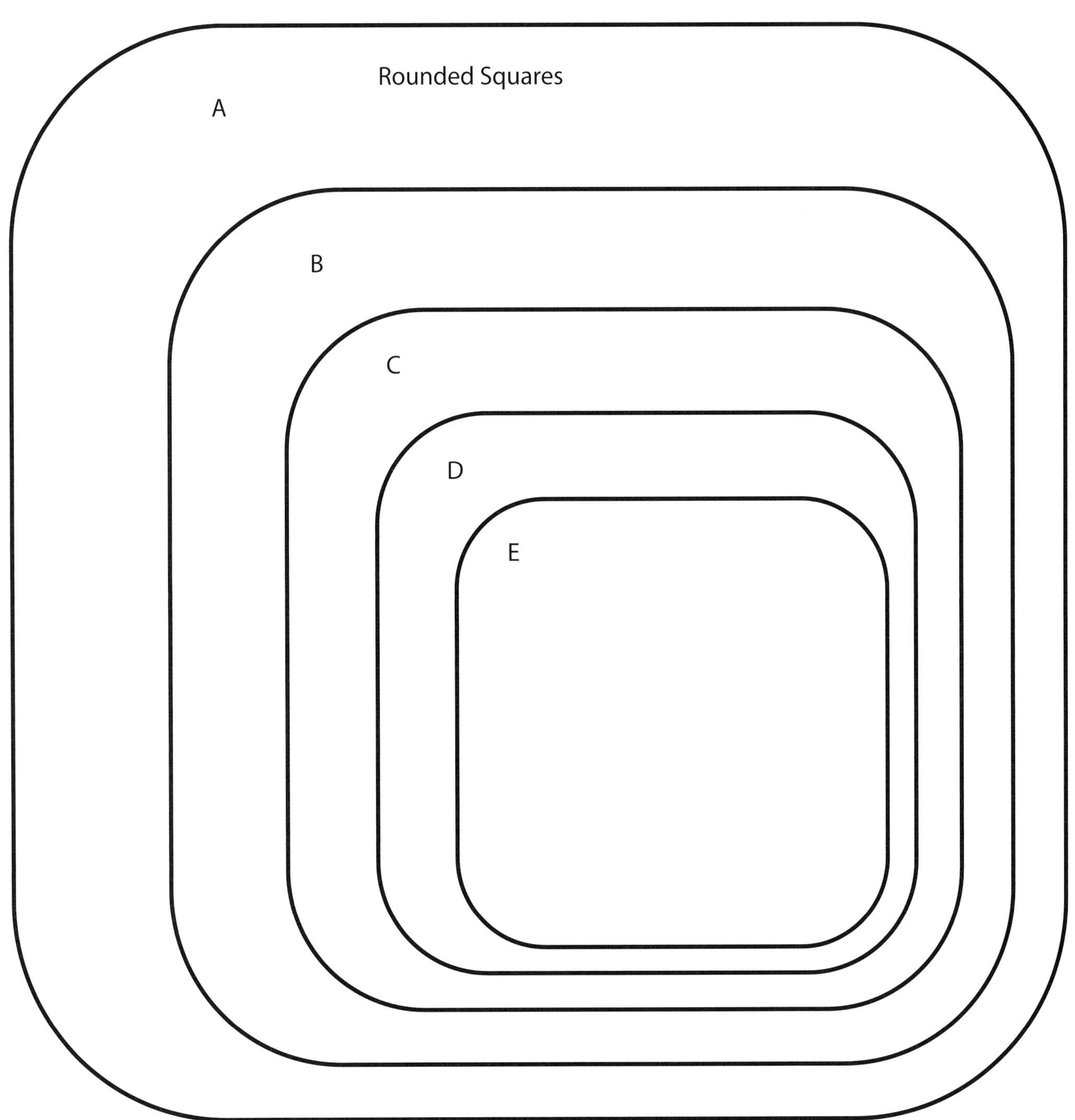
Rounded Squares
A
B
C
D
E

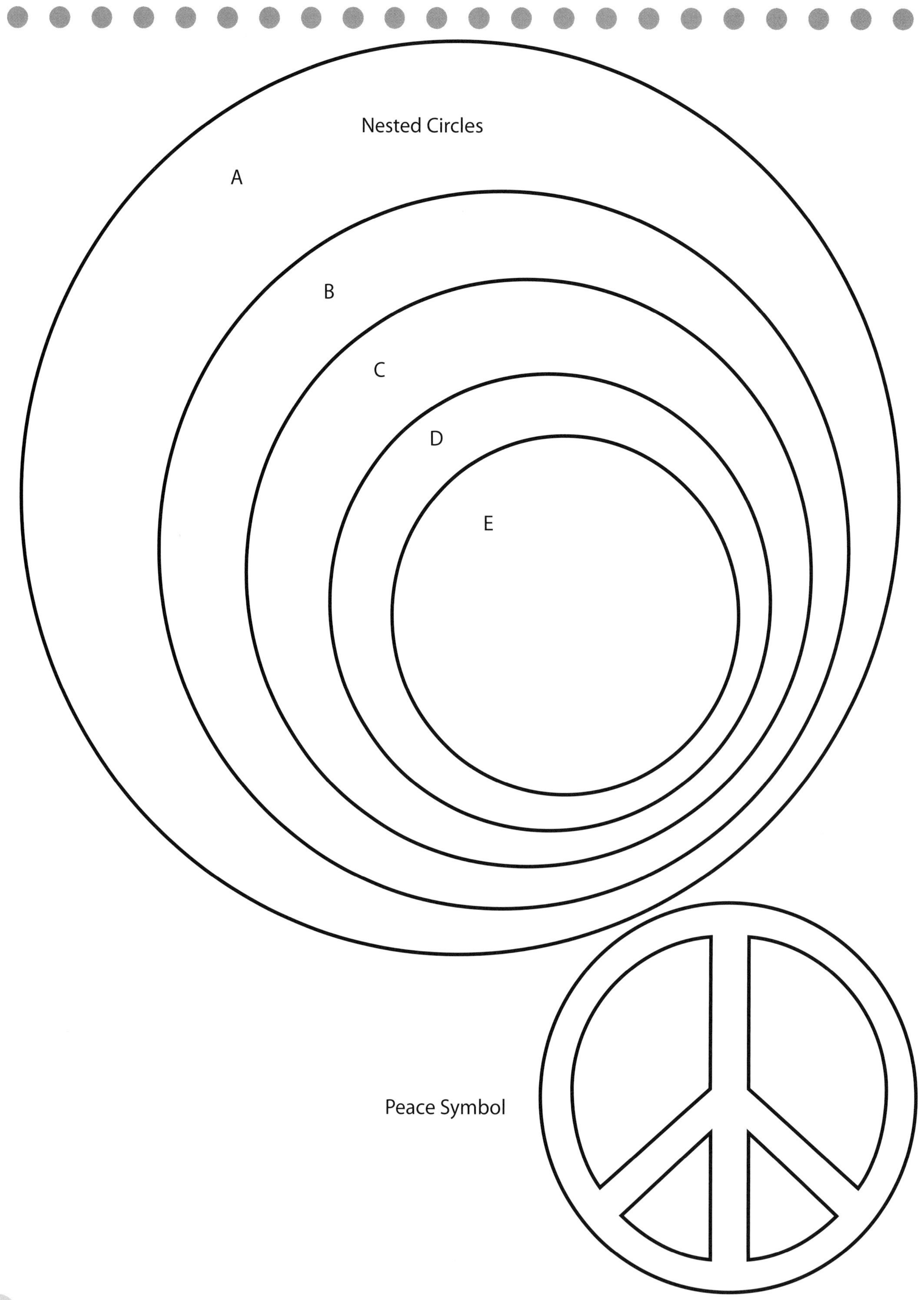
Nested Circles
A
B
C
D
E
Peace Symbol

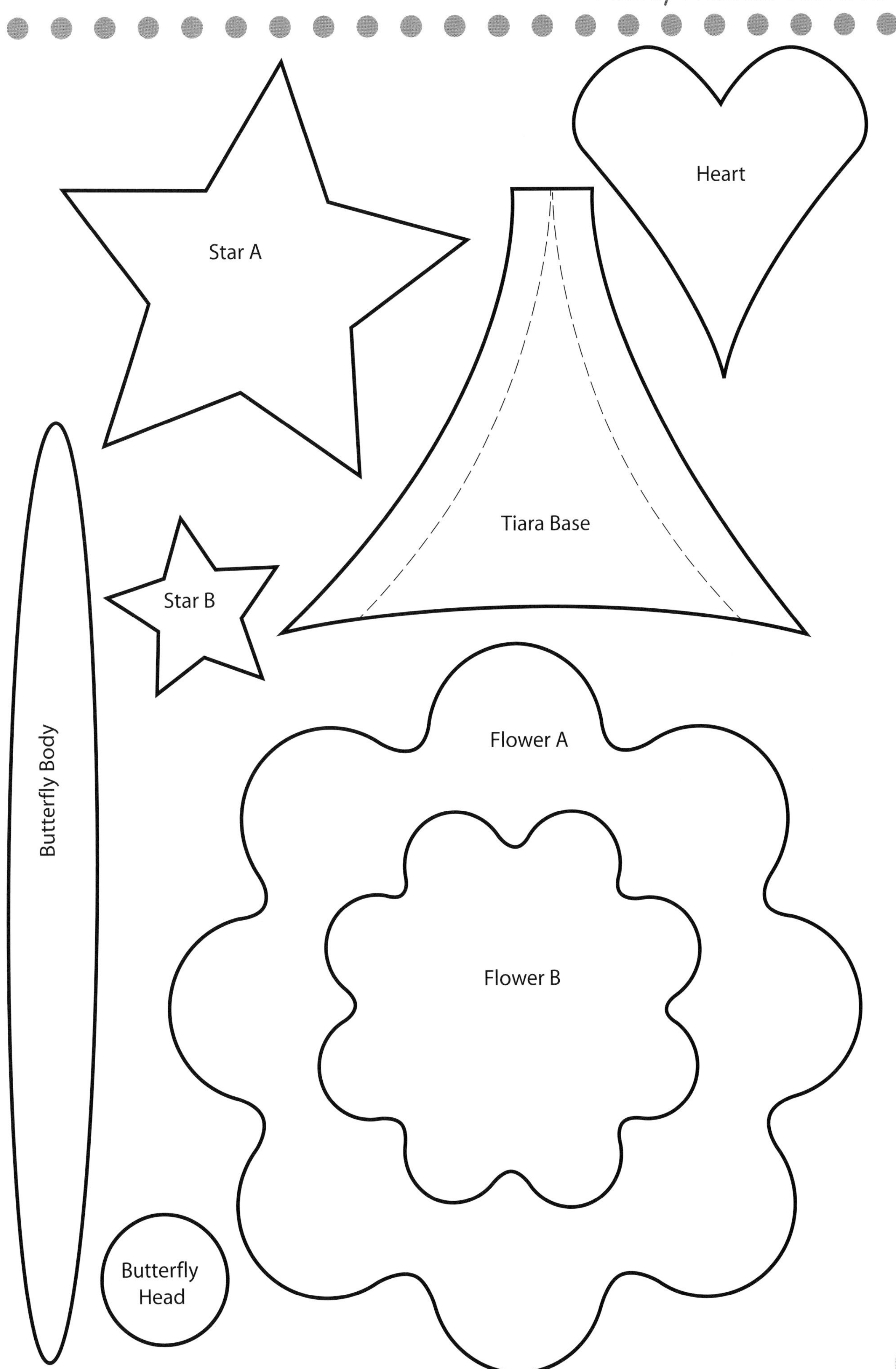
Star A
Heart
Tiara Base
Star B
Butterfly Body
Flower A
Flower B
Butterfly Head

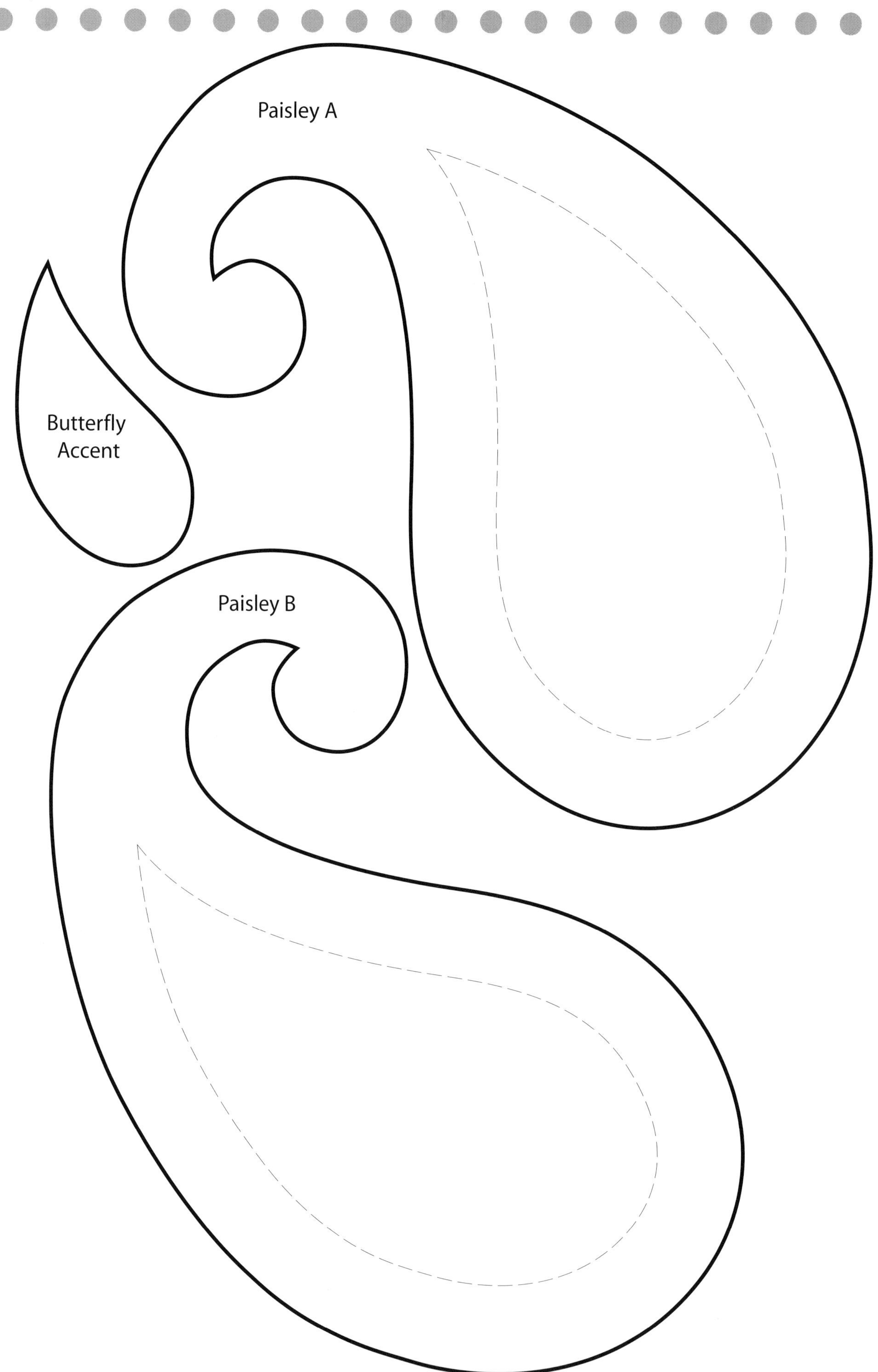
Paisley A
Butterfly
Accent
Paisley B

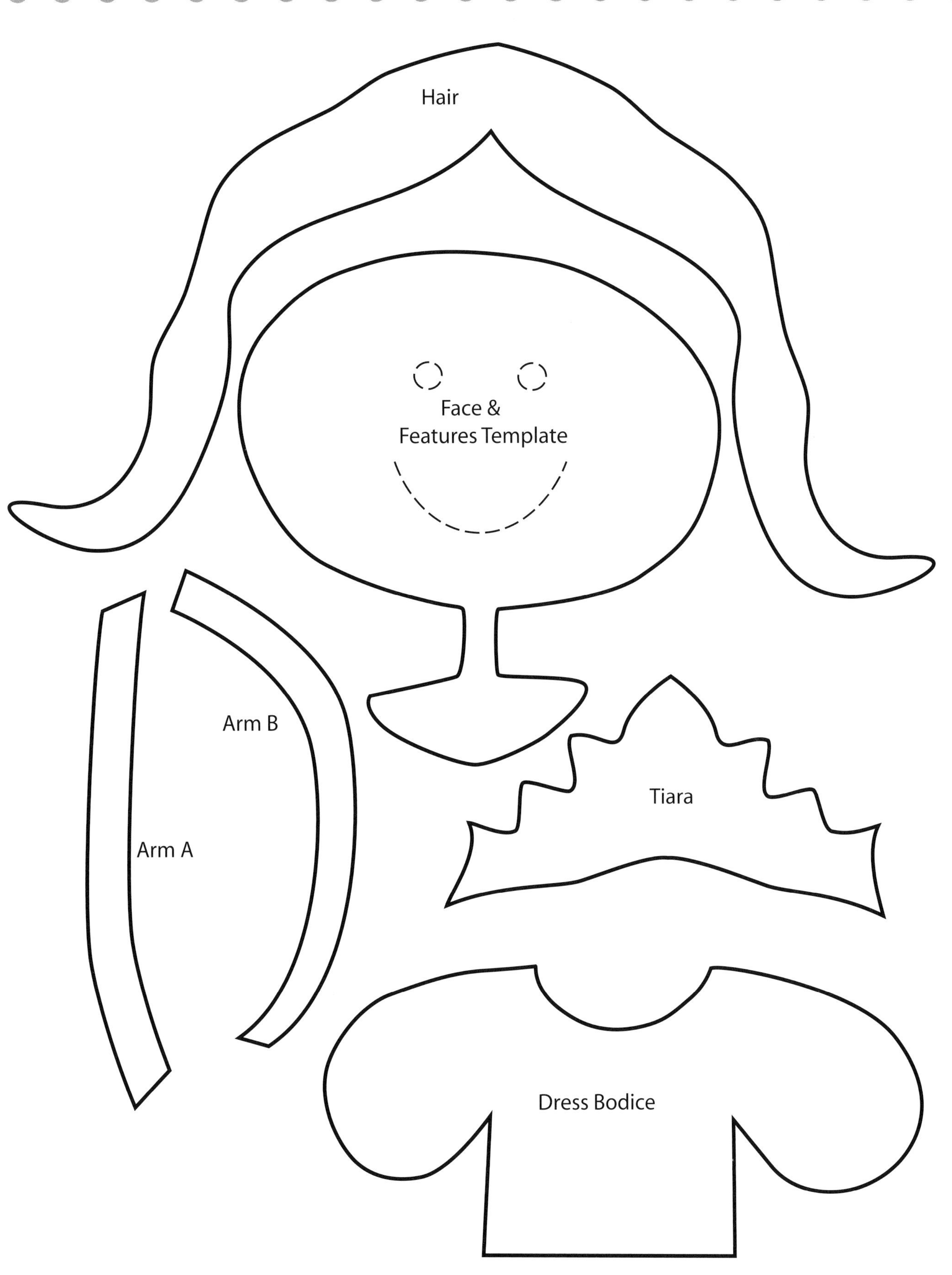
Hair
Face &
Features Template
Arm B
Arm A
Tiara
Dress Bodice

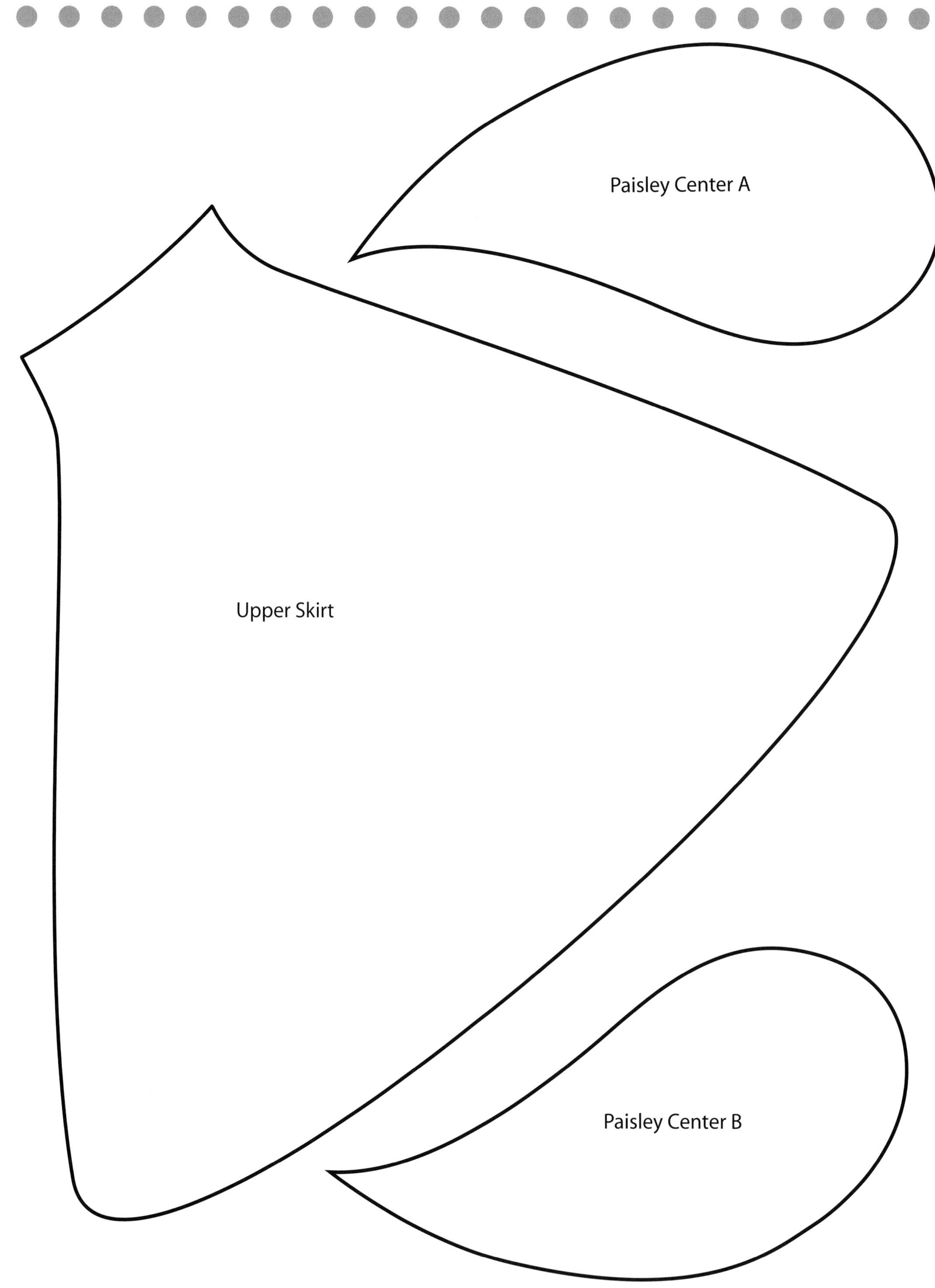
Paisley Center A
Upper Skirt
Paisley Center B

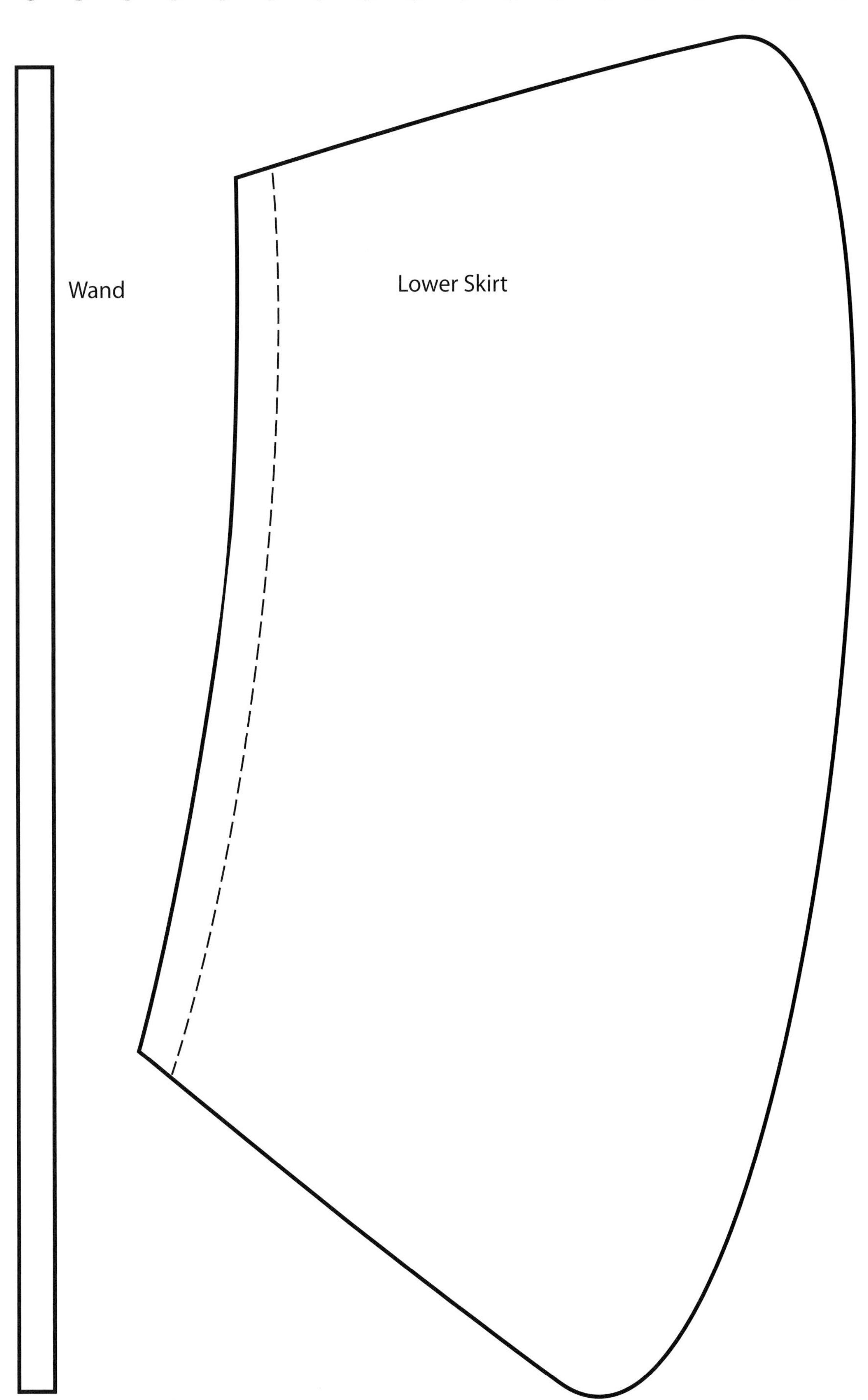
Wand
Lower Skirt

Paisley Princess Layouts

Use these layouts as guides for pattern placement to build a motif. For full-size layouts copy at 400%, keeping in mind that many of these layouts are larger than a standard sheet of paper. To download full-size layouts go to www.landauerpub.com.

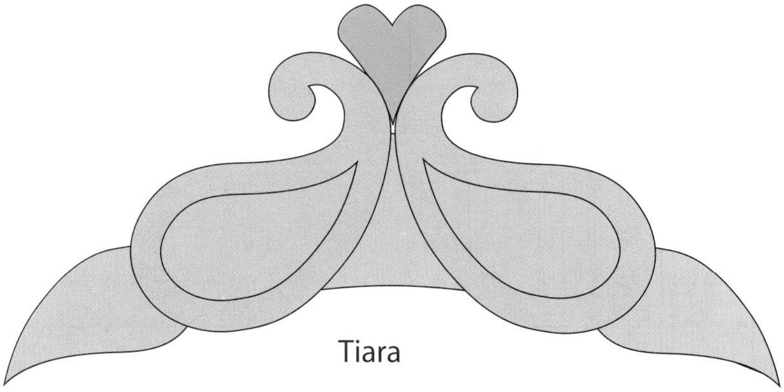

Tiara

Flower

Princess

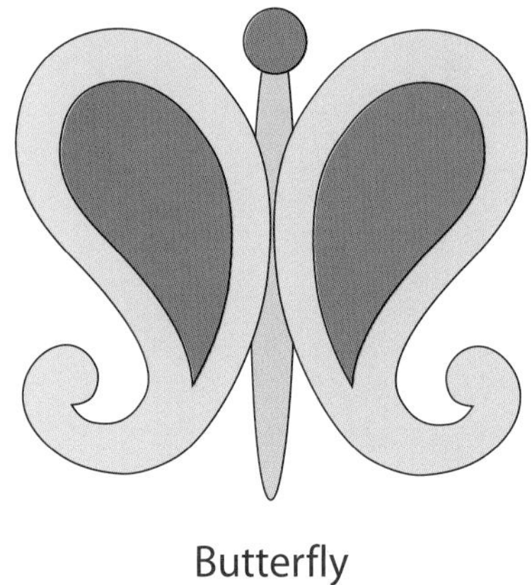

Butterfly

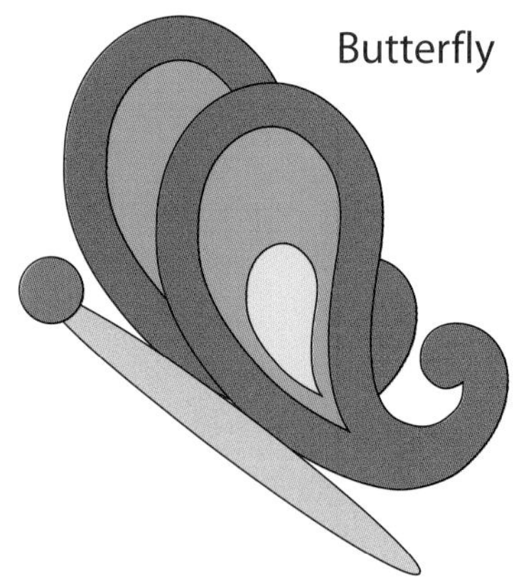

Butterfly

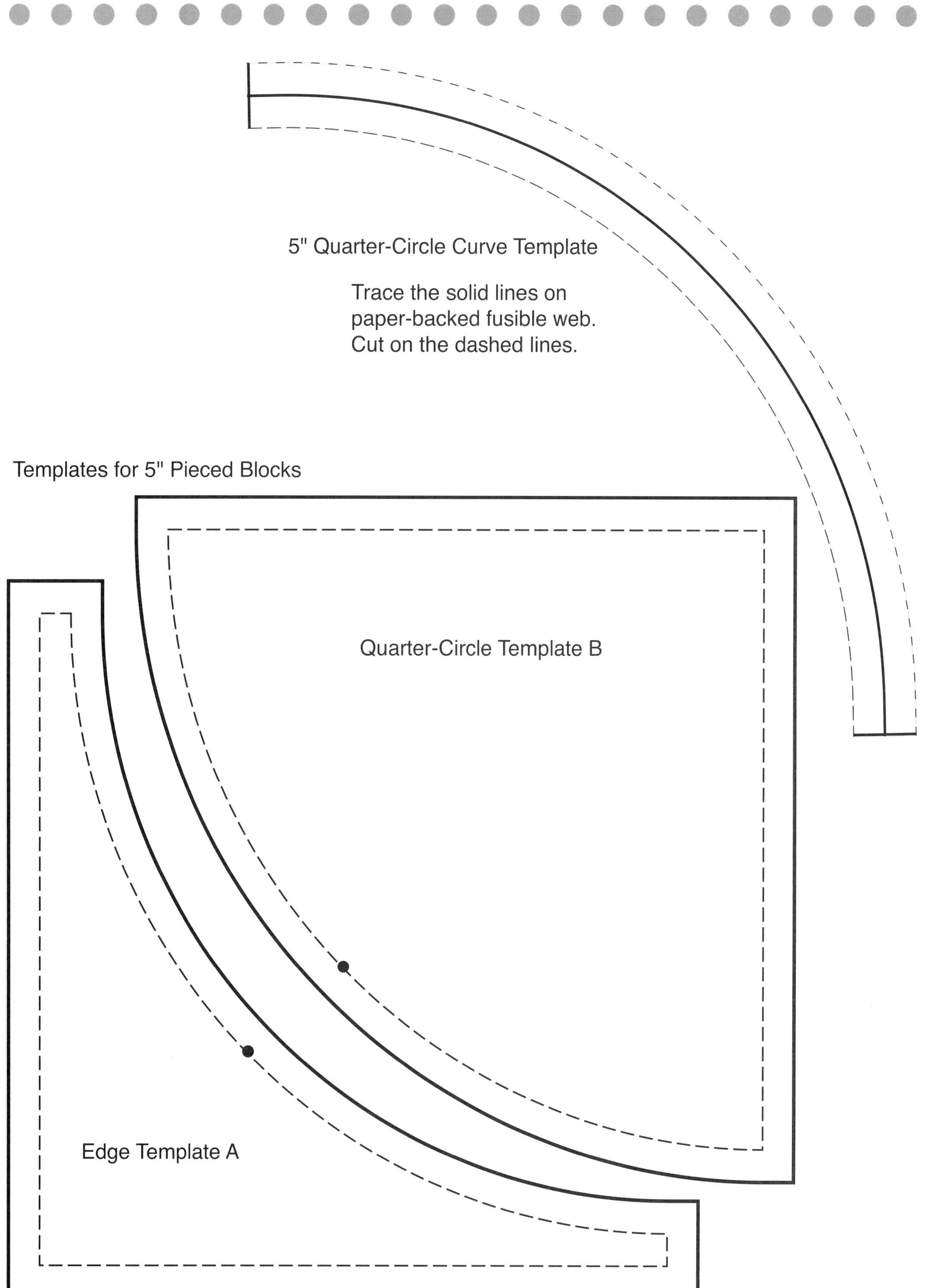
5" Quarter-Circle Curve Template
Trace the solid lines on paper-backed fusible web. Cut on the dashed lines.
Templates for 5" Pieced Blocks
Quarter-Circle Template B
Edge Template A

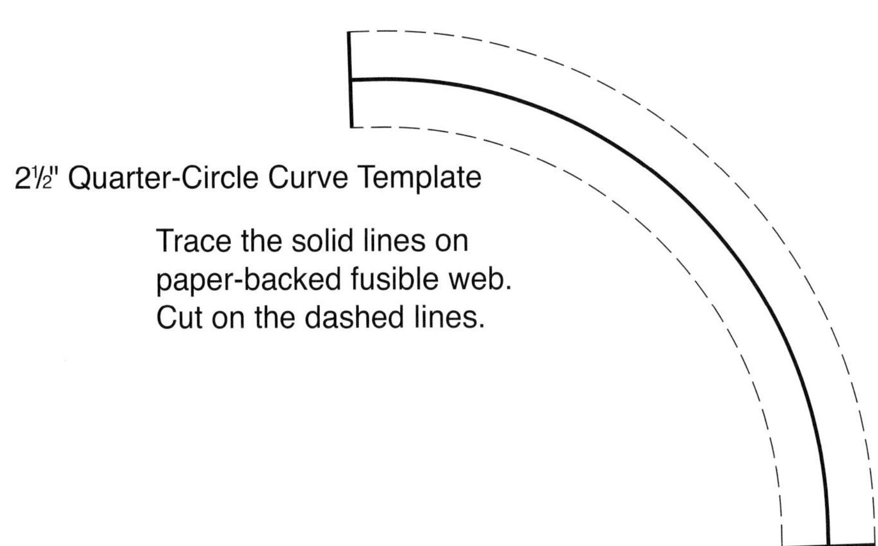

Templates for 2½" Pieced Blocks

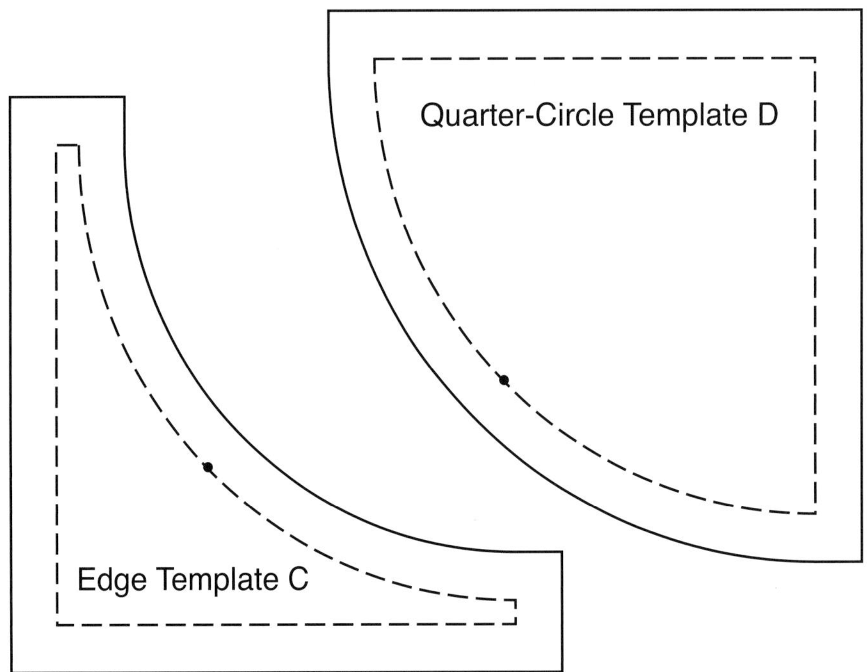

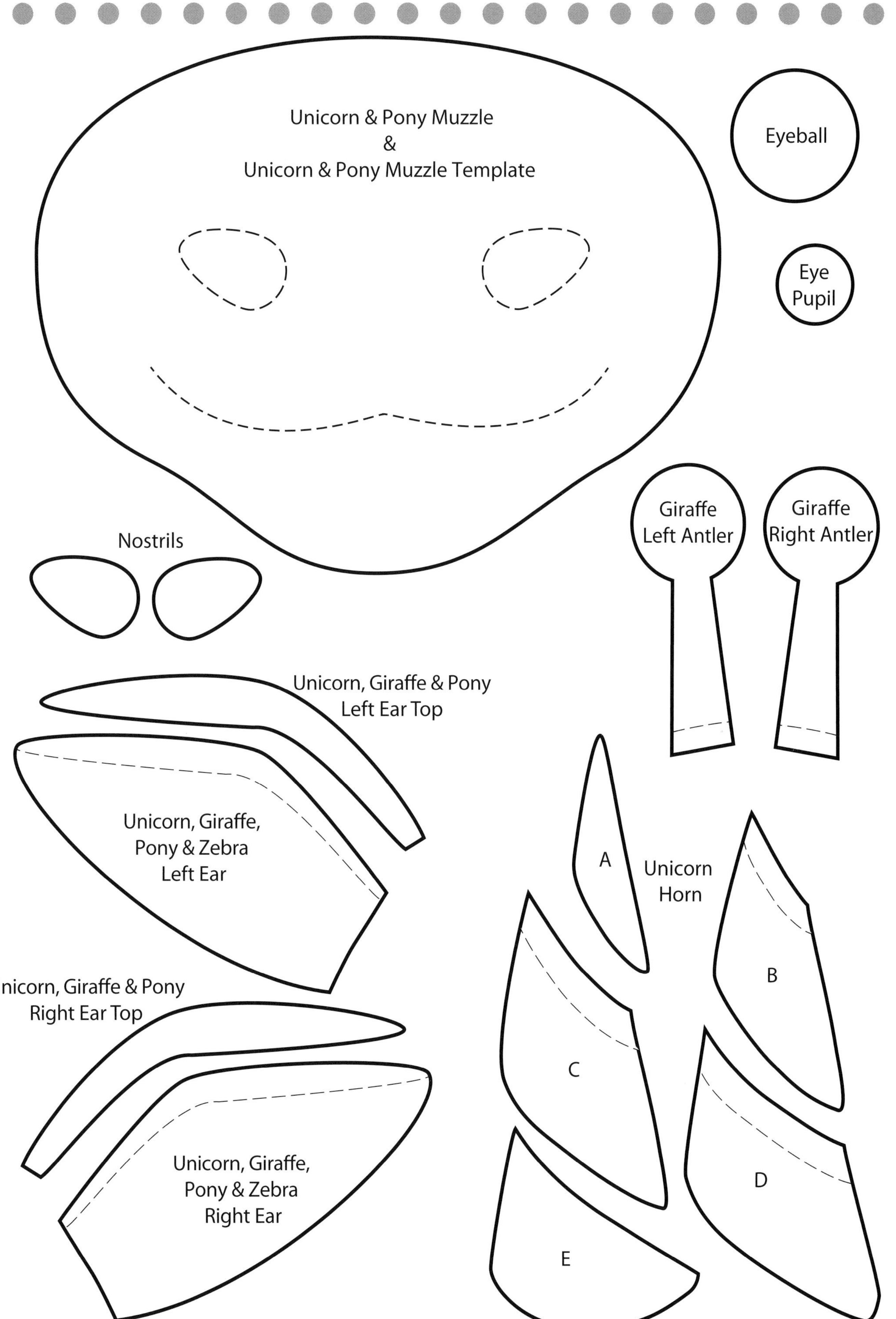
Unicorn & Pony Muzzle
&
Unicorn & Pony Muzzle Template
Eyeball
Eye
Pupil
Giraffe
Left Antler
Giraffe
Right Antler
Nostrils
Unicorn, Giraffe & Pony
Left Ear Top
Unicorn, Giraffe,
Pony & Zebra
Left Ear
A
Unicorn
Horn
B
C
Unicorn, Giraffe & Pony
Right Ear Top
D
Unicorn, Giraffe,
Pony & Zebra
Right Ear
E

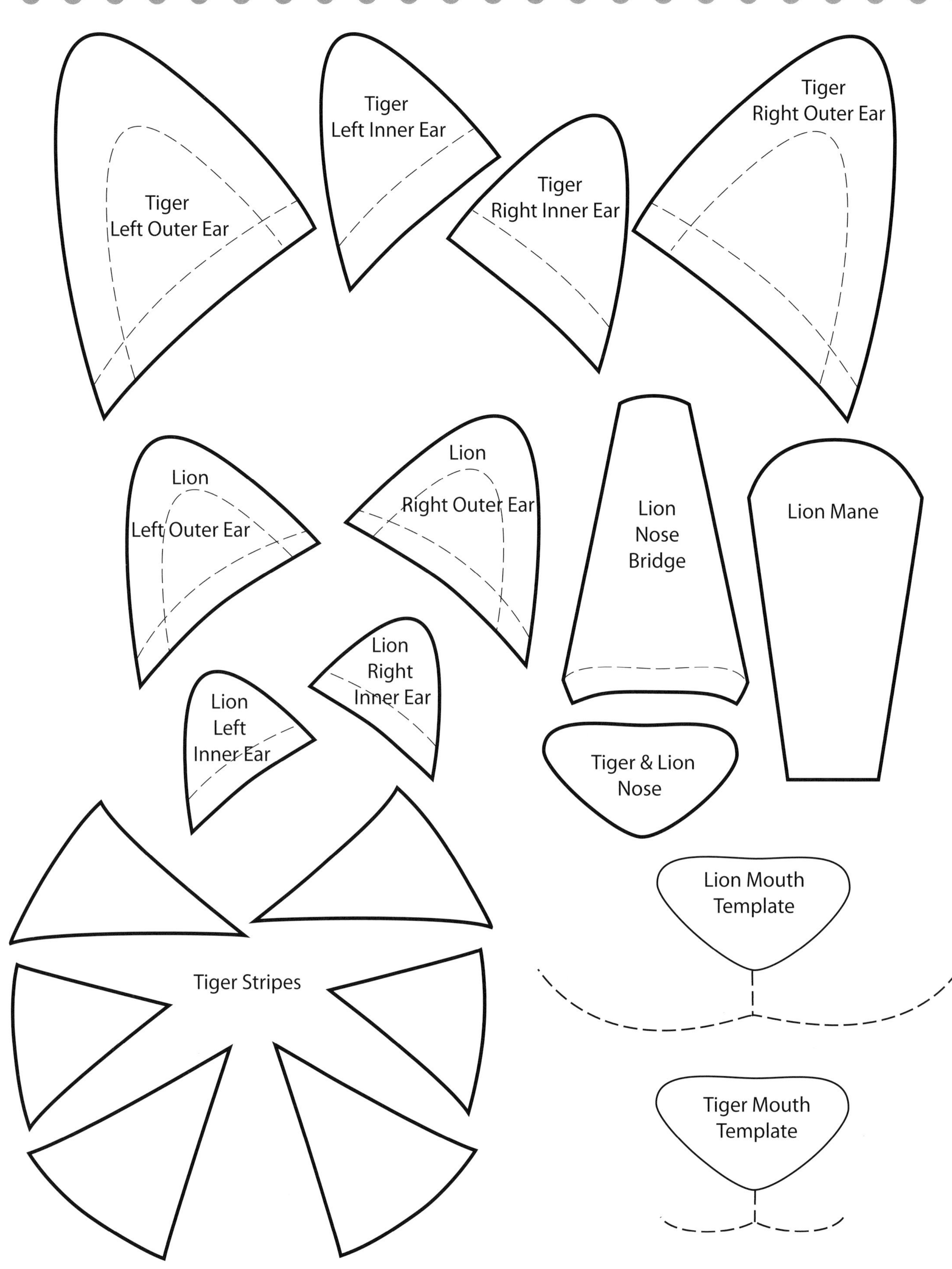
Tiger
Left Outer Ear
Tiger
Left Inner Ear
Tiger
Right Inner Ear
Tiger
Right Outer Ear
Lion
Left Outer Ear
Lion
Right Outer Ear
Lion
Nose
Bridge
Lion Mane
Lion
Right
Inner Ear
Lion
Left
Inner Ear
Tiger & Lion
Nose
Lion Mouth
Template
Tiger Stripes
Tiger Mouth
Template

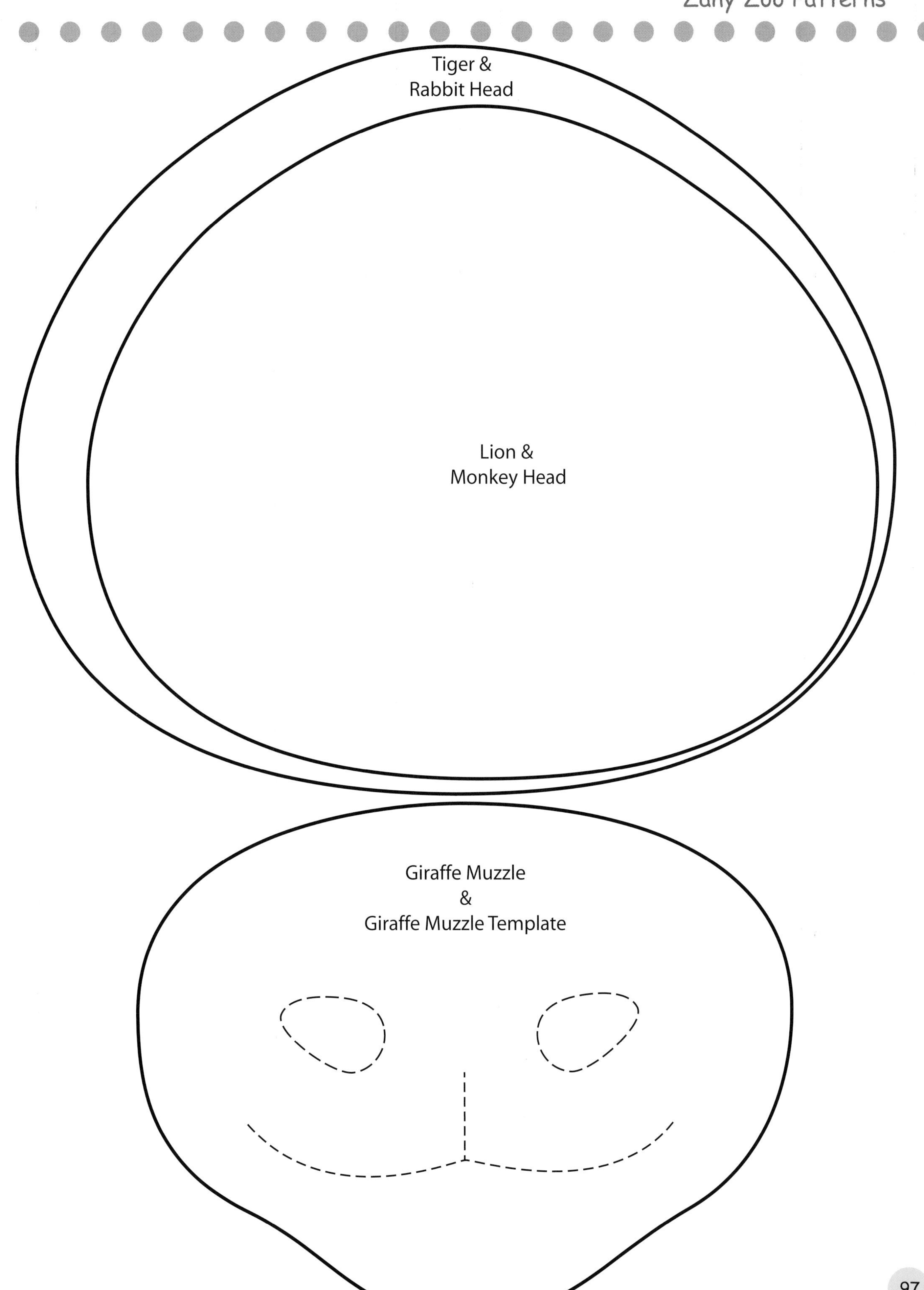
Tiger &
Rabbit Head
Lion &
Monkey Head
Giraffe Muzzle
&
Giraffe Muzzle Template

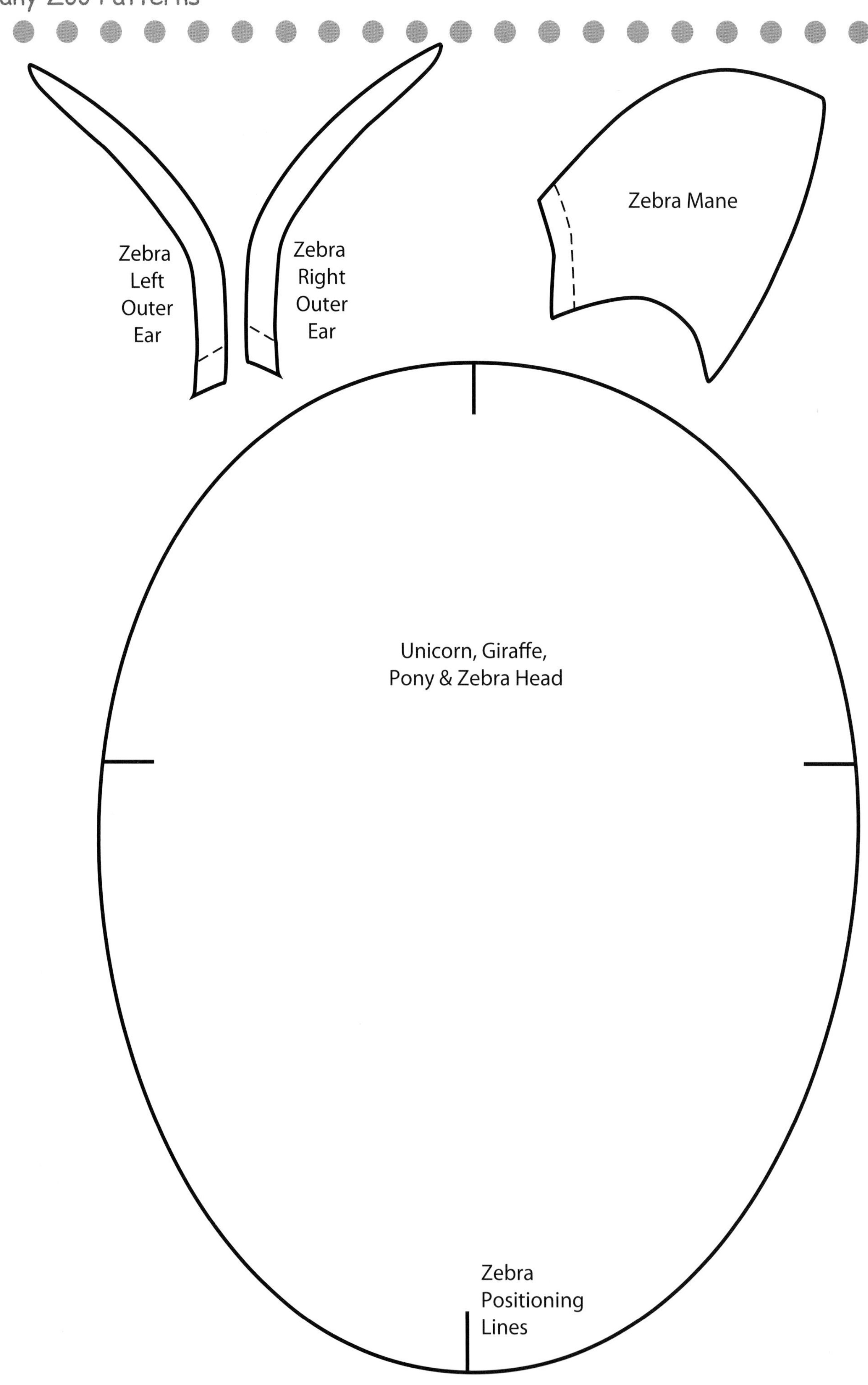
Zebra
Left
Outer
Ear
Zebra
Right
Outer
Ear
Zebra Mane
Unicorn, Giraffe,
Pony & Zebra Head
Zebra
Positioning
Lines

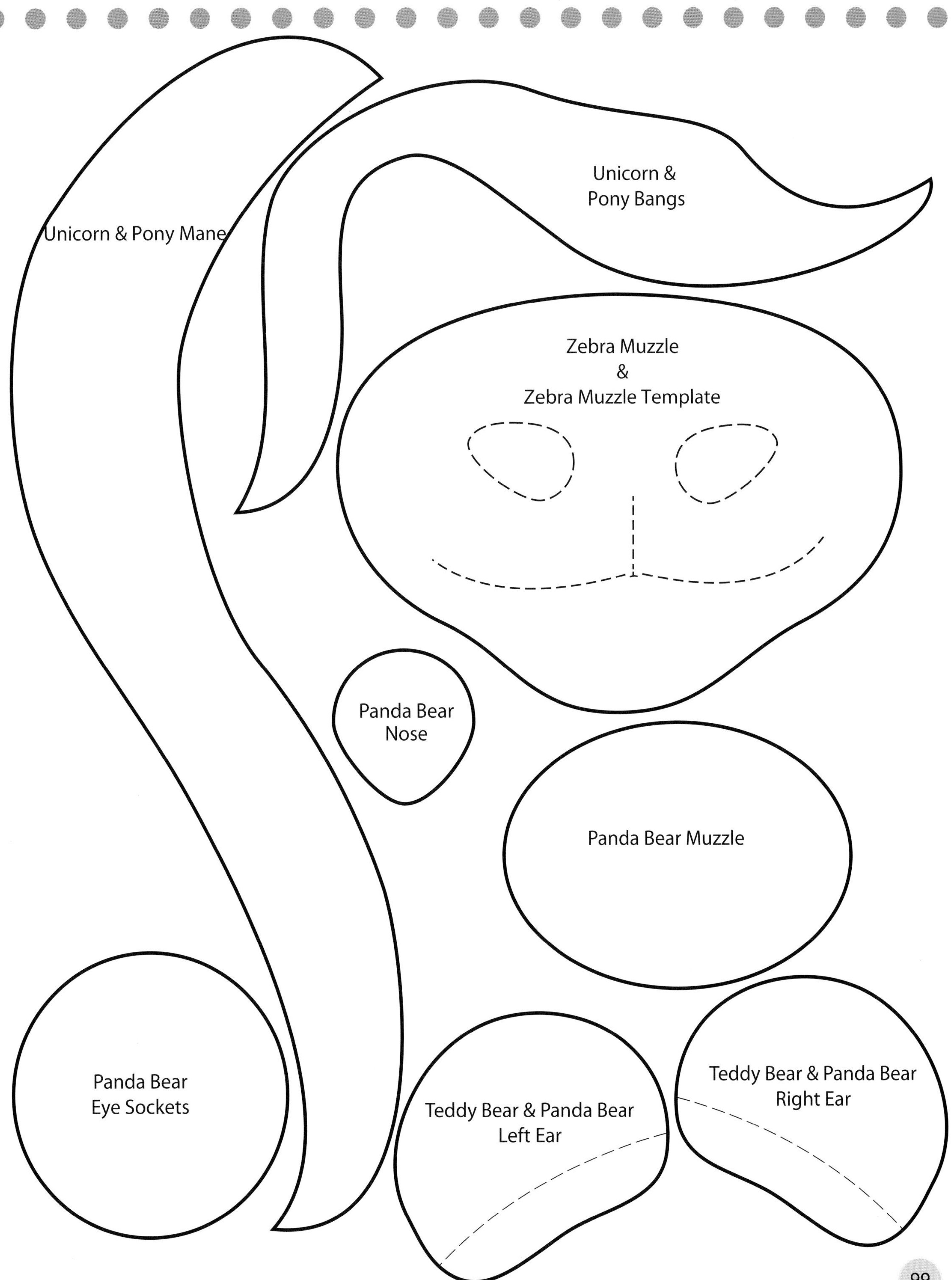
Unicorn & Pony Mane
Unicorn &
Pony Bangs
Zebra Muzzle
&
Zebra Muzzle Template
Panda Bear
Nose
Panda Bear Muzzle
Panda Bear
Eye Sockets
Teddy Bear & Panda Bear
Left Ear
Teddy Bear & Panda Bear
Right Ear

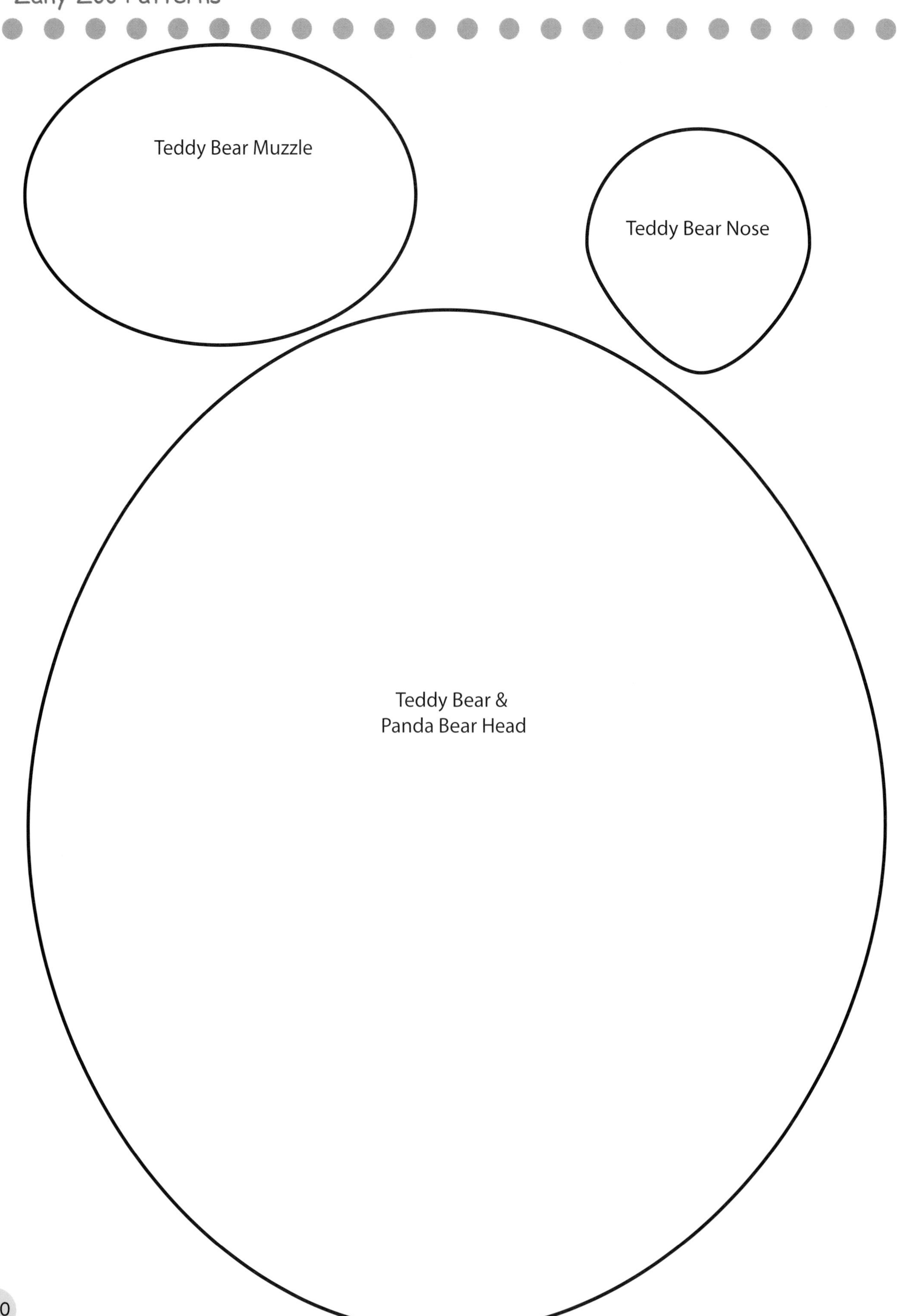
Teddy Bear Muzzle
Teddy Bear Nose
Teddy Bear &
Panda Bear Head

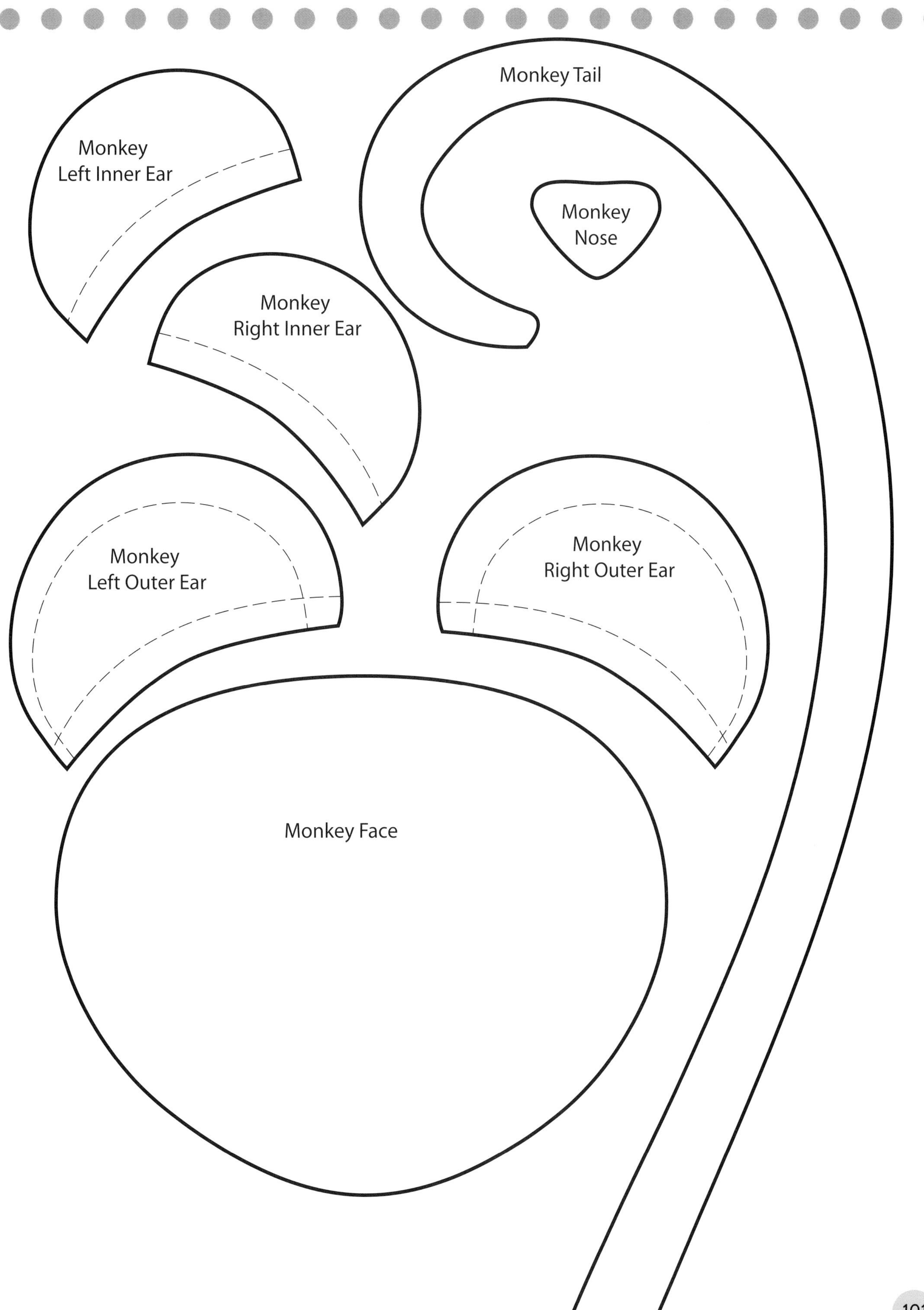
Monkey Tail
Monkey
Left Inner Ear
Monkey
Nose
Monkey
Right Inner Ear
Monkey
Left Outer Ear
Monkey
Right Outer Ear
Monkey Face

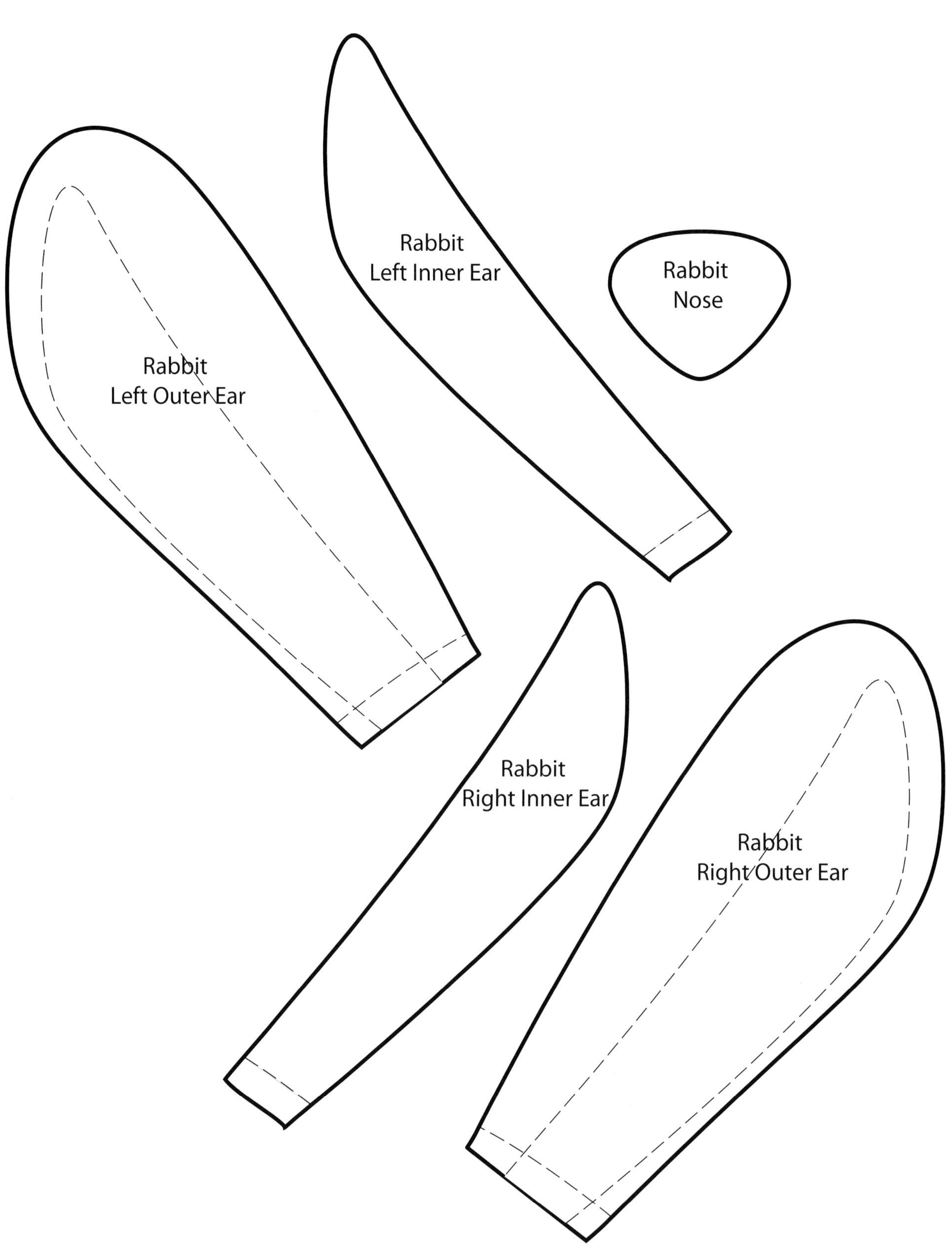
Rabbit
Left Inner Ear
Rabbit
Nose
Rabbit
Left Outer Ear
Rabbit
Right Inner Ear
Rabbit
Right Outer Ear

Use these layouts as guides for pattern placement to build a motif. For full-size layouts copy at 400%, keeping in mind that many of these layouts are larger than a standard sheet of paper. To download full-size layouts go to www.landauerpub.com.

A B C D
F G H
CONSTRUCTIO

other things
you need to know

The following pages include the equipment and supplies I rely on to make comfy kids quilts. You may already have some of these supplies on hand. Hopefully the information in this section will show you some additional uses for a few of them. My favorite techniques for preparing appliqué, stitching, embellishing, and printing photos for kids quilt projects are detailed. And a finishing section covers quilting, binding and labeling.

equipment and supplies

If you are planning on purchasing supplies, first decide which techniques you would like to practice, and then purchase the best equipment and supplies you can afford.

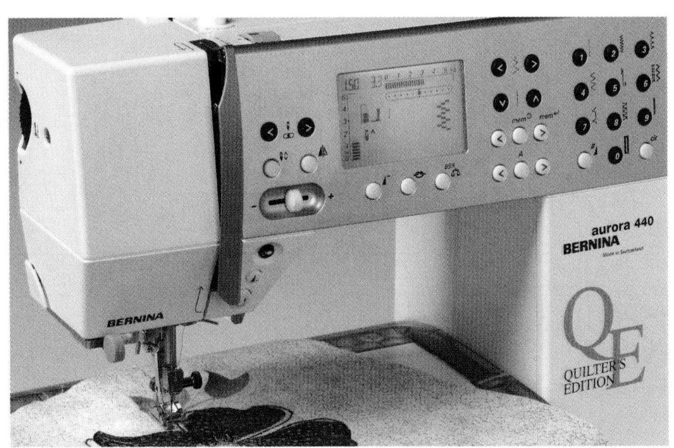

A Sewing Machine in good working order is needed for piecing. The capability to zigzag stitch is a must for machine appliqué. Clean your machine to remove any lint, oil it regularly, and have it serviced as recommended by the manufacturer.

For machine appliqué, the following sewing machine features are recommended:

Top Tension

An adjustable upper thread tension in combination with an adjustable bobbin tension is important for any stitching. It may be especially necessary for decorative threads as well as lightweight rayon and polyester threads.

Stitch Width and Length

An adjustable stitch length and width allows you to make decorative choices in your zigzag, blanket, and machine appliqué stitches.

Needle Position

An adjustable needle position feature allows you to find the best combination of needle position and presser foot for guiding your stitching.

It is helpful to have a needle up/needle down function. Leaving the needle down at the end of a stitch allows you to pivot your work without it slipping out of place.

Presser Feet

Having a variety of presser feet for your sewing machine will ensure accurate piecing and machine appliqué. The following feet are recommended:

A 1/4" Foot is essential for sewing accurate seams.

An Open Toe Embroidery or Appliqué Foot

An Open Toe Embroidery or Appliqué Foot has a wide opening in front so you can see the stitching. It also has a groove molded in the bottom to allow the thread build-up from stitching to pass under it smoothly.

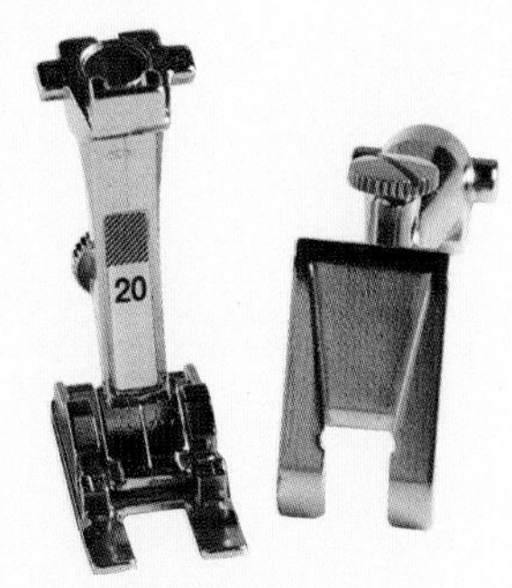

Free-Motion or Darning Foot

A Free-Motion or Darning Foot allows the material to move freely under the foot for free-motion, straight and zigzag stitching. I recommend using this foot during quilting to stitch around and add texture to the appliqué.

Walking Foot

A Walking Foot is designed to move the upper fabric while the feed dogs move the bottom fabric. This allows for stitching without any puckers or bunched fabric. I recommend using it during piecing, quilting, and binding.

Machine Needles

Machine Needles are available in different sizes and quality. These needles, which include sharp, metallic, topstitch, and embroidery, are each manufactured for a specific job. They vary in sharpness of the point, size of the eye, and thickness of the blade. Select the smallest needle with the appropriate point for your project. Purchase the best quality needles and replace as necessary.

Scissors come in many styles, sizes, and qualities. Purchase the best quality you can afford. Some scissors have a knife edge or a very fine serrated edge. Sharp points or blunt tips make some jobs easier. A handle grip of flexible material or a spring release will make cutting easier. Use smaller scissors for trimming threads while a project is in the machine. Keep a pair of good quality blunt tip scissors that will cut fabric for the kids in your sewing room

Threads are available in many different colors, textures, and fiber contents. Thread spools are generally marked with the size and ply of the thread. The higher the size number, the smaller the thread diameter. The ply number indicates the number of fine yarns that are twisted together. Spools are also marked with the fiber content.

- **Cotton thread** comes in a wide range of colors making it easy to match to almost any appliqué fabric. Spools for the sewing machine range from fine embroidery 80/2 to 12/2. For most machine appliqué techniques, use 60/2 or 50/2 embroidery thread. If heavier stitching is desired, use 30/2 or 12/2.
- **Monofilament nylon or polyester threads** are size .004 mm and are usually labeled "invisible". Use this thread for invisible machine appliqué stitching. You may already have this thread on hand for invisible machine quilting. The sheen of the thread varies by brand so experiment for the look you prefer.
- **Rayon and polyester threads** are usually 40- to 30-weight. These threads, which are my favorite for decorative stitching, often have more luster than cotton and therefore provide a more decorative touch to projects. This luster blends well with more shades of appliqué fabric and does not have as defined an edge as cotton after stitching. This can be a plus when blending colors in decorative stitching. Man-made fibers also come in more decorative threads such as metallic and ribbon-like polyester film.
- **Bobbin thread** comes in a variety of sizes and fiber content. When working with 30- to-60-weight cotton, rayon or polyester threads, match the bobbin thread to the top thread and you should not have to adjust the top tension to get a perfect stitch. The bobbin thread should not show on top of the appliqué. If you will be changing top thread color frequently, it is more convenient to choose one thread for the bobbin. However, this may cause the top tension to need to be adjusted. For decorative stitching where there is a heavy build up of thread, such as satin zigzag and free-motion embroidery, a fine polyester 80/2 to 120/2 bobbin-weight thread works well. Because these threads are so thin, you may have to lower the top tension to almost 0 and thread the bobbin thread through the pigtail, if your bobbin case has one.

Fabric used for appliqué is usually 100 percent cotton. There is a wide variety of color, print and thread count choices in quilt shops and fabric stores. Any fabric used for piecing can also be used for appliqué. For fusible appliqué or appliqué with turned under edges, any cotton fabric may be used. Keep in mind that fabric with a low thread count may fray and be more difficult to work with. Fabric with a high thread count, such as a batik, will keep a crisp edge for fusible and turned under appliqué.

- If your project is going to be washed you will want to test fabrics for colorfastness. If one fabric is prewashed, then all fabrics should be prewashed. Iron the fabrics before using for any type of appliqué. Do not spray with starch or sizing as this may prevent fusible web and freezer paper from adhering when preparing pieces for appliqué.
- When selecting fabrics for an appliqué project, look for contrast in value among the colors. For most appliqué pieces, I like tone on tone prints, solids, or an overall pattern such as dots. These will add texture to your quilt without having a pattern getting in the way of the shape of the appliqué pieces.
- For wallhangings or quilts that will not be washed, any fabric can be used. Silks, polyesters, and rayons will have different stitching and care requirements. Make a sample with each fabric to find which method of appliqué works best. Test the method, thread, needles, and stitches before using in a project.

Paper-Backed Fusible Web

Paper-backed fusible web has revolutionized appliqué for many quilters. Trace the design directly onto the paper backing, fuse to the wrong side of fabric, cut out the appliqué shape, remove paper, fuse to the background fabric and you are ready to stitch. There are no pins getting in the way and the stitching is generally done by machine. Fusible web brands differ regarding the iron temperature and time requirements for pressing so follow manufacturer's instructions. Test several brands to find the one you like. Paper-backed fusible web is also available in multiple weights, each designed for a different purpose. For appliqué to have a soft traditional appearance, use the lightest weight paper-backed fusible web available and window it. See page 110.

Stabilizers

Stabilizers are essential for many machine appliqué techniques. The thin layer of adhesive in fusible web acts as a stabilizer for fine and narrow satin zigzag stitching. For bias edges, wider stitches and stitching through one or two layers of fabric, use a temporary stabilizer and a wooden hoop.

- Temporary Sheet Stabilizers can be carefully torn, cut, ironed, or washed away. For sheet stabilizers place a piece the full size of your background or just the size necessary to fit behind the appliqué. Use pins or temporary spray adhesive to hold in place. Carefully remove stabilizer after stitching.
- Wooden or plastic embroidery hoops are especially useful for decorative stitching on appliqué. They keep the background taut while stitching. For machine stitching use a hoop in addition to a temporary stabilizer for maximum hold. Look for a 7"-8" round hoop with a strong screw mechanism since the appliqué may have several layers of fabric and stitching.

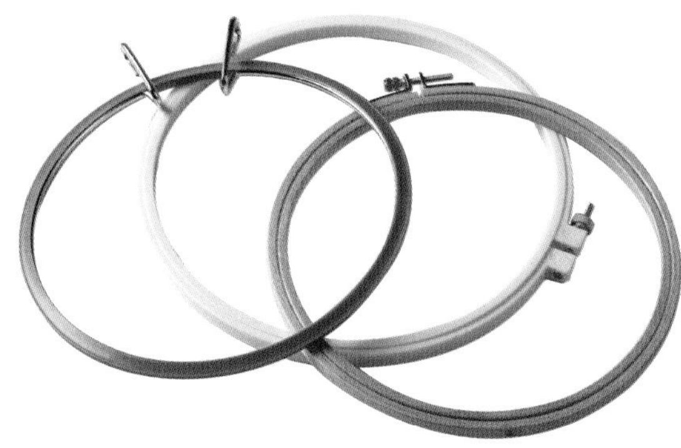

Non-stick Pressing Sheets

Non-stick Pressing Sheets are indispensable when working with paper-backed fusible web. Care needs to be taken to prevent your iron and ironing board from getting sticky with adhesive. You can protect the work surface with Teflon® or non-stick coated woven or plastic sheets, or cooking parchment paper. See Arranging Appliqué on page 113 for other uses for non-stick pressing sheets.

Marking Tools come in many varieties, colors, and tip widths. A ultra-fine tip permanent marker can be used to trace patterns onto paper-backed fusible web and freezer paper. It dries almost immediately and will not smudge.

Tissue or Tracing Paper can be useful for marking the appliqué motif if working on a dark background. See page 113. It can also be used for making a stitching template for mouths and other stitched lines. See page 121.

preparing appliqué

All the appliqué quilts in this book have been made using paper-backed fusible web, which is my favorite method. If you would rather use a turned edge, I have also included instructions for that type of preparation.

Preparing Fused Appliqué

Paper-backed fusible web can be used for any machine appliqué. It is especially useful for shapes with intricate edges that would be difficult to turn under. All the patterns in this book are separate pieces rather than motifs. I have added placement lines which are indicated by dashed lines.

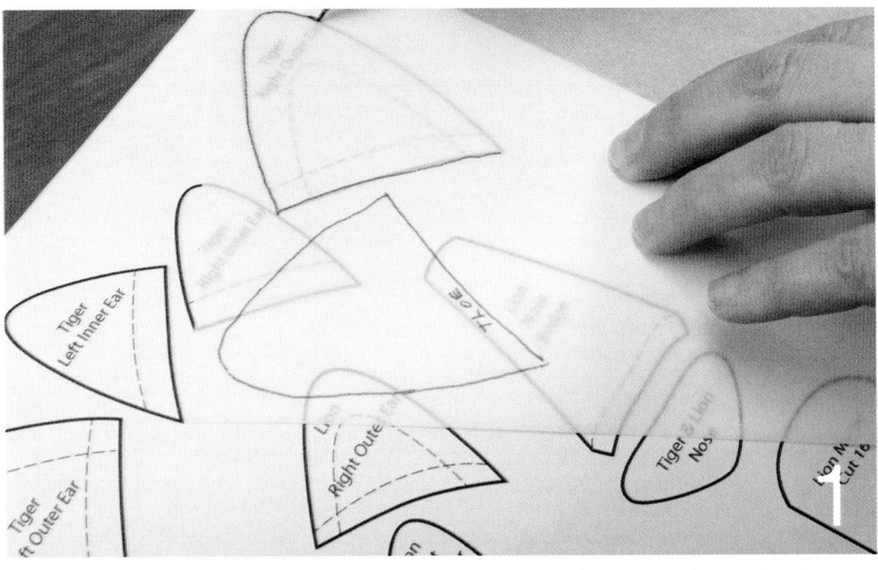

Place lightweight paper-backed fusible web with paper side up on the appliqué pattern. Using an ultra-fine tip permanent marker or pencil, trace each pattern piece onto the paper side of the fusible web. Mark the pattern name near an edge of the pattern.

Trace appliqué pieces that will be cut from the same fabric about 1/8" apart.

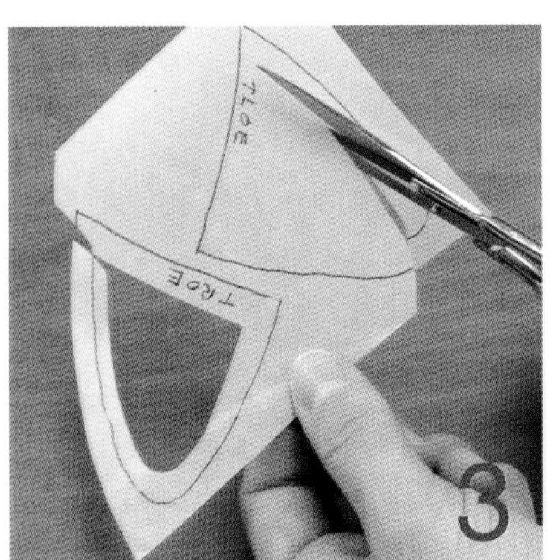

If desired, remove the fusible web from the center of the larger pattern pieces. Cut through an outer edge into the center of the pattern. Cut out the center leaving a scant 1/4" inside the traced line. This makes the appliqué center softer to the touch and in appearance. This technique is frequently called "windowing".

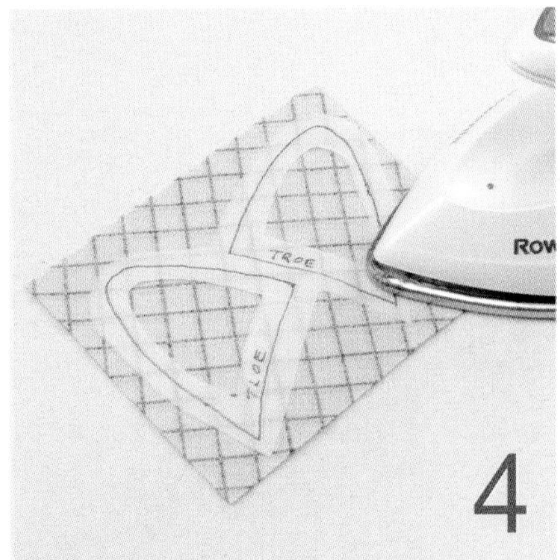

Cut away excess fusible web about 1/8" from the traced lines. Fuse patterns to wrong side of fabric, following manufacturer's directions. Each brand of fusible web comes with instructions detailing pressing times and iron temperatures.

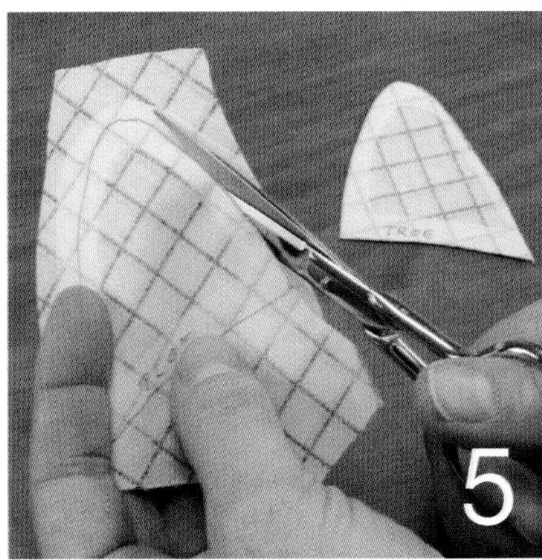

Cut out fused appliqué pieces on the traced line. Do not remove paper backing until just before arranging the pieces for pressing to background. This preserves the pattern name. If you are working with hand-dyed or batik fabrics where it is hard to tell right from wrong side of fabric, this will also help tell which side has the glue. It also prevents a gummed up iron surface.

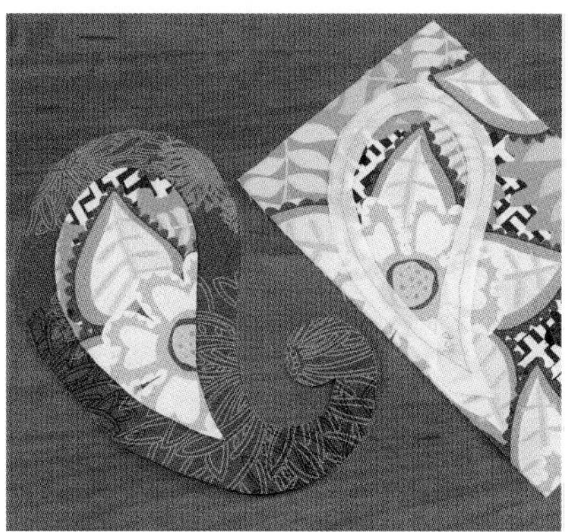

Fussy Cutting

If you want a specific printed motif on an appliqué piece, trace the pattern piece separately and window. Windowing allows you to see the area desired in the appliqué piece. Turn fabric over and fuse the pattern to the wrong side in the chosen position.

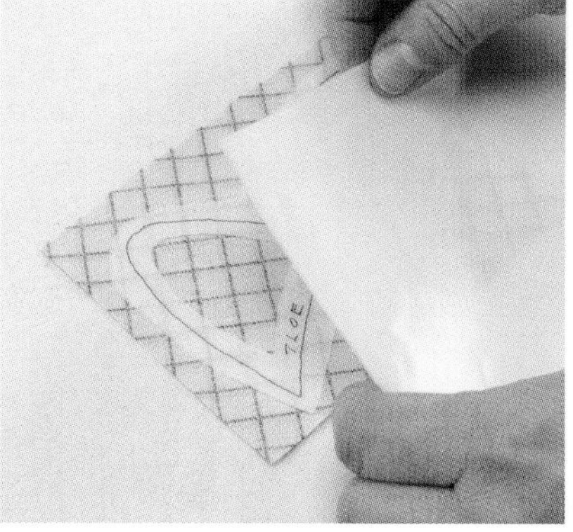

Protect Your Iron and Ironing Board

To prevent fusible web from gumming up the surface of your iron, cover the appliqué patterns with a non-stick pressing sheet or parchment paper. Do this as you are pressing fusible web to wrong side of appliqué fabric and as you are arranging the layout.

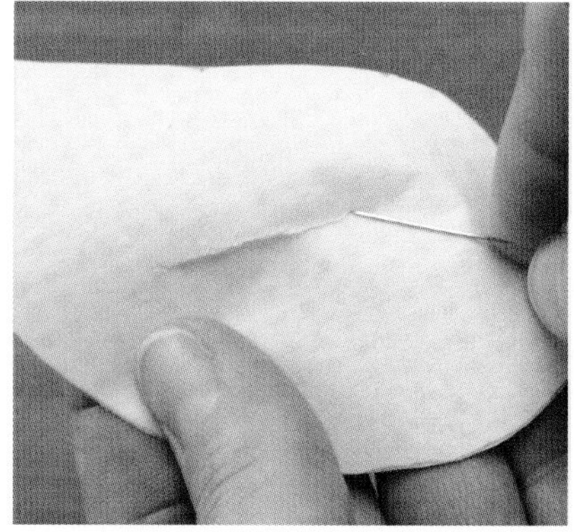

Removing Paper Backing

If you do not window the fusible web, it may be difficult to find an edge of the paper to pull away. Drag a pin across the center of the fused pattern to cut the paper but not the fabric. This provides an edge of paper to pull to remove it.

To Prevent Creases

Press all fabric to remove wrinkles and creases before preparing appliqué pieces. Any creases will be almost impossible to remove after fusing.

Lining Light Colors

When light colored appliqué pieces overlap darker colors, the darker color often shadows through. To prevent this, line the appliqué pieces with the same color or white fabric. Notice how the area of overlap of the skin fabric and white fabric does not have a ghost of the stripe fabric showing through.

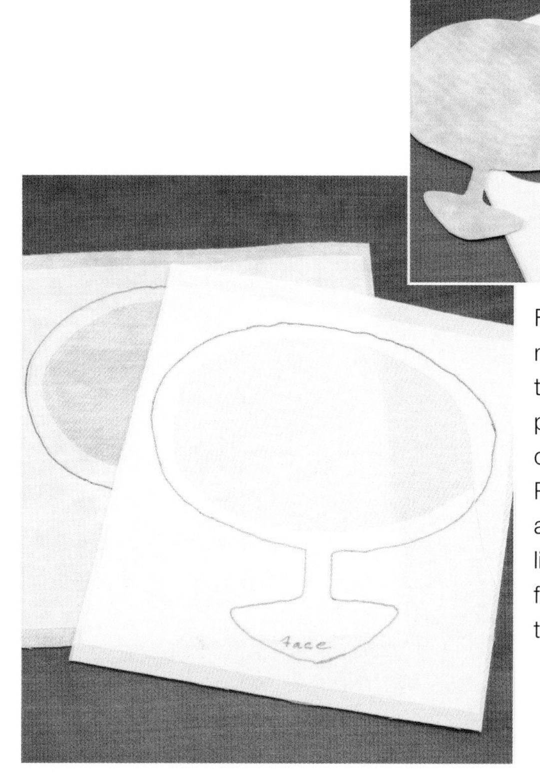

For paper-backed fusible web, make duplicate tracings. Fuse the pattern pieces in the same position on the same size pieces of appliqué and lining fabric. Remove paper from the appliqué and fuse it to the lining fabric, lining up the patterns and the fabric edges. Cut out using the traced line on the fusible web.

Preparing Turned Edge Appliqué

The following instructions cover only one of many methods using freezer paper templates for turning the edges of appliqué pieces. The freezer paper templates are removed before stitching making this turned under method very versatile. It can be used with any invisible, blanket, or zigzag machine stitching. For more options refer to the book *Appliqué The Basics and Beyond*.

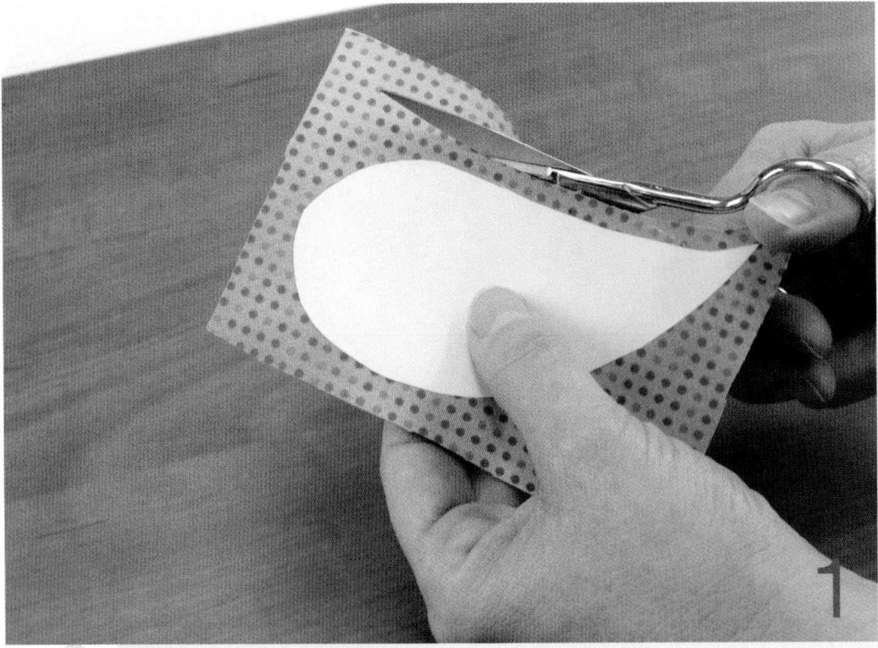

1

Place freezer paper shiny-side up on the appliqué pattern. Using an ultra-fine tip permanent marker, trace individual pattern pieces. Mark with pattern name. This is for reference while building appliqué designs. Cut shapes out on the traced lines. Press freezer paper pattern shiny-side down on right side of the fabric. Form a seam allowance by trimming the fabric a scant 1/4" outside the freezer paper pattern.

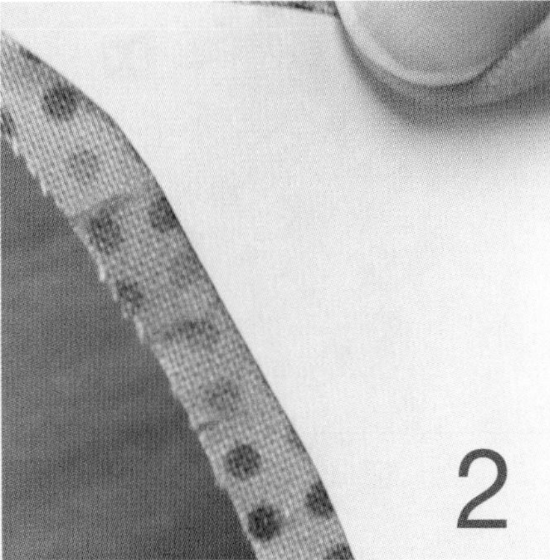

2

Clip inside curves around the edge of the appliqué shape. When clipping inside curves, clip approximately halfway to the edge of the pattern. Clip inside points straight into the point to within one thread of the pattern.

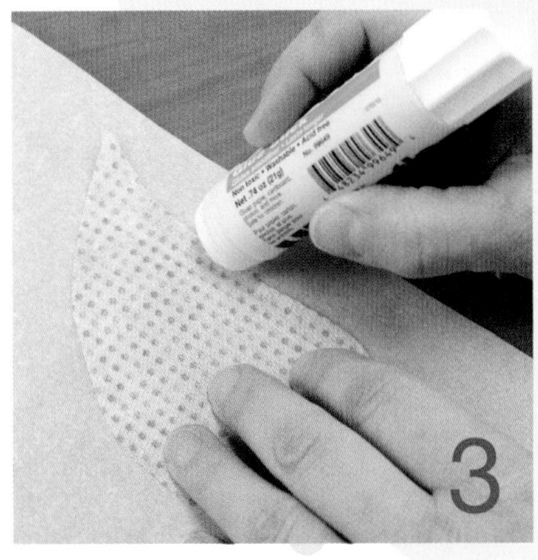

3

Using a washable glue stick, apply glue to the seam allowance edge on the wrong side of the fabric. Do not apply glue to the underlap sections. To protect table surface, place appliqué pieces on parchment or freezer paper.

4

Working in small sections, use the edge of the freezer paper template as a guide to finger press the glued fabric seam allowance to the wrong side, away from the freezer paper. Place the tip of your thumb on top and index finger underneath the shape as you turn the seam allowance. On outside curves make very small tucks, or pleats, in the fabric. Apply more glue if necessary. Do not press the seam allowance on edges that underlap.

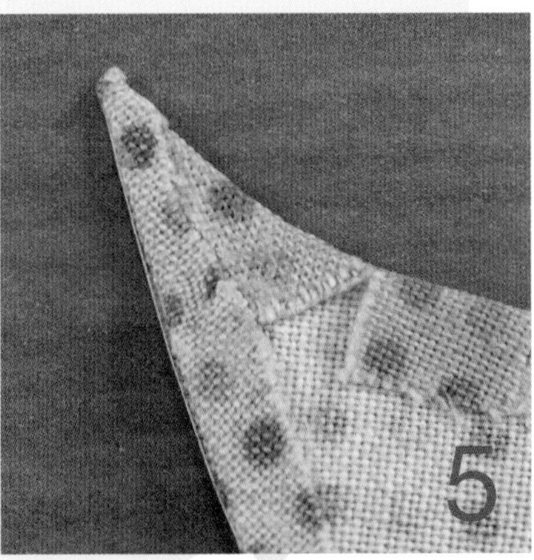

5

For a sharp outside point, finger press the excess fabric at the tip directly over the point. Press the seam allowance in on one side, trimming if necessary. Press the other side's seam allowance in, making a sharp point. Allow glue to dry completely. Remove freezer paper before layering or stitching.

arranging appliqué

There are various methods for arranging appliqué pieces on the background fabric. It is always easiest if you use a full-size appliqué placement layout. For fusing, I prefer to arrange and fuse a multi-piece motif before applying it to the background fabric.

Arranging motifs and pieces on backgrounds

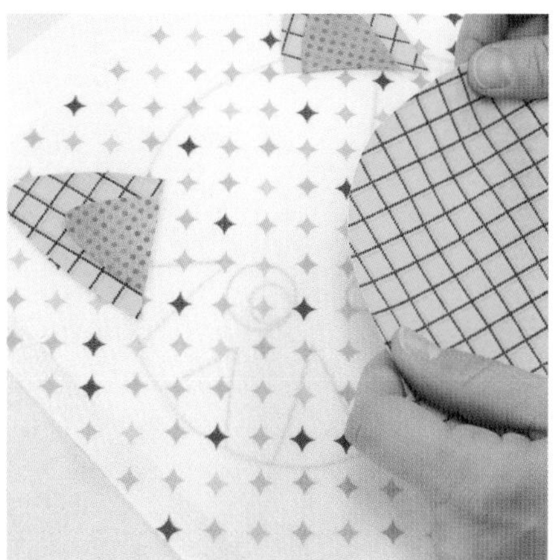

For light backgrounds place the light background on top of the full-size appliqué placement layout. Arrange the appliqué pieces, including already fused motifs, on the background.

For medium to dark backgrounds make a pattern layout overlay. Cut a piece of tissue or tracing paper approximately the size of the appliqué background. Place on top of the full-size appliqué placement layout and trace the design.

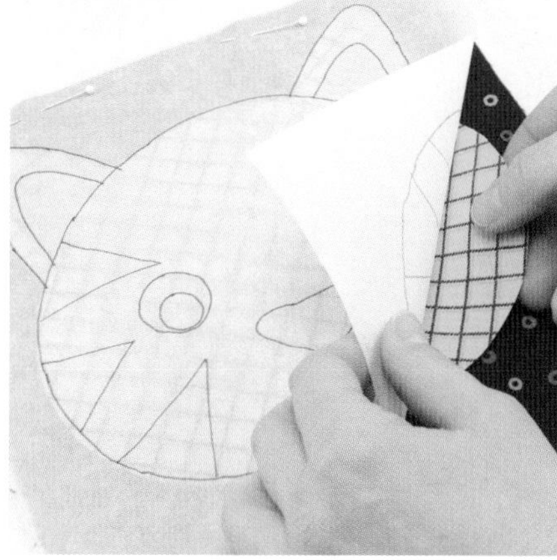

Position the pattern overlay on the background block and pin or tape to the top or one side. Arrange the appliqué pieces, including already fused motifs, a few at a time on the background by lifting overlay slightly and sliding the pieces in place.

Printing a full-size appliqué placement layout

All patterns in this book are full size but the appliqué placement layouts on pages 84, 92, and 103 are shown at 25%. Use them as reference for pattern placement to build a motif. For ease in stitching facial features, I have included full-size templates along with the patterns. For full-size layouts copy at 400%, keeping in mind that many of these layouts are larger than a standard sheet of paper. To download full-size layouts go to www.landauerpub.com.

Pre-fusing appliqué motifs

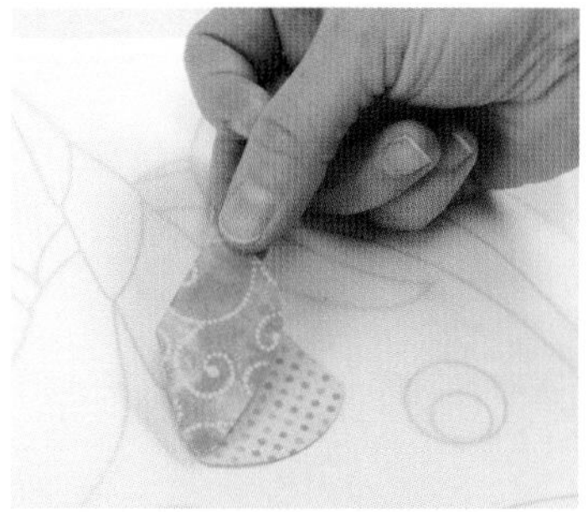

1. Place the full-size appliqué placement layout under a non-stick pressing sheet. Remove paper backing from appliqué pieces. Arrange the bottom layer of pieces on the pressing sheet. Tack into place with a hot iron as you build the design.

2. Continue adding appliqué pieces and press to form the design. Cool and remove the fused design from non-stick sheet.

Arranging small pieces on top of a fabric motif

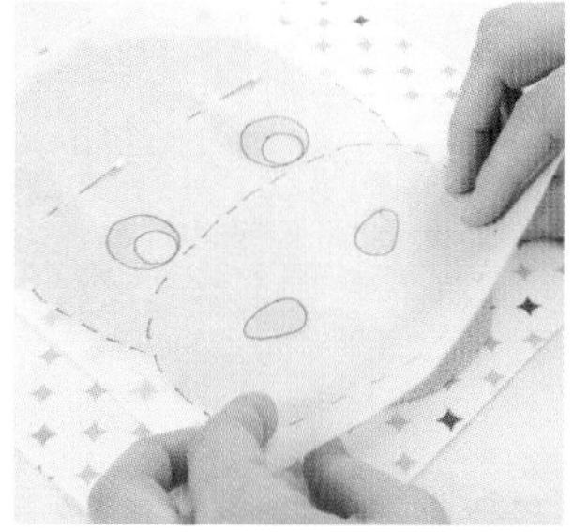

1. Make a small overlay of the section needed, such as the face of an animal.
2. Pin the overlay to motif and arrange the pieces under the tracing.

Arranging one layer at a time

Pin the overlay to the top of the background fabric. Lift overlay slightly and arrange the bottom most pieces. Remove overlay; stitch in place. Reposition overlay, add the next layer of appliqué pieces and stitch. Continue until stitching is finished.

machine stitching appliqué

When stitching appliqué pieces to a background, there are many choices. You can use anything from an almost invisible to very decorative stitch.

Beginning the Stitching

When beginning the stitch, bring the bobbin thread to the top. Take one stitch and pull on the top thread to bring the bobbin thread loop up. This will prevent a snarl or knot of thread on the back of your appliqué.

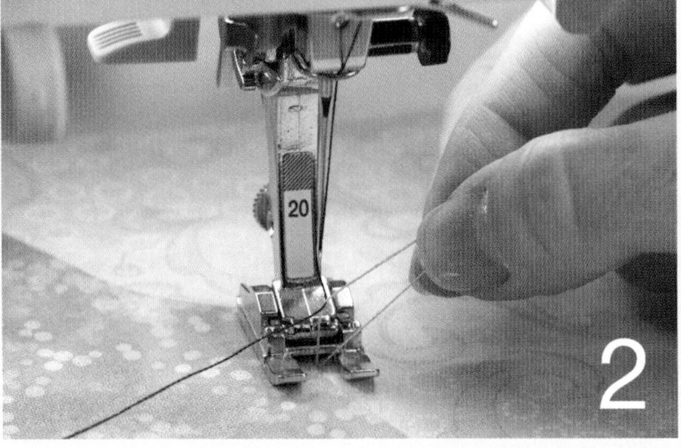

Pull on the loop of bobbin thread to pull the tail to the top. Take a few short locking stitches and start stitching.

Ending the Stitching

To end the stitching, take a few very short stitches to lock the threads. Pull stitching away from the needle and clip beginning and ending thread tails.

Note: The beginning and ending stitching is the same for all machine stitching in this section.

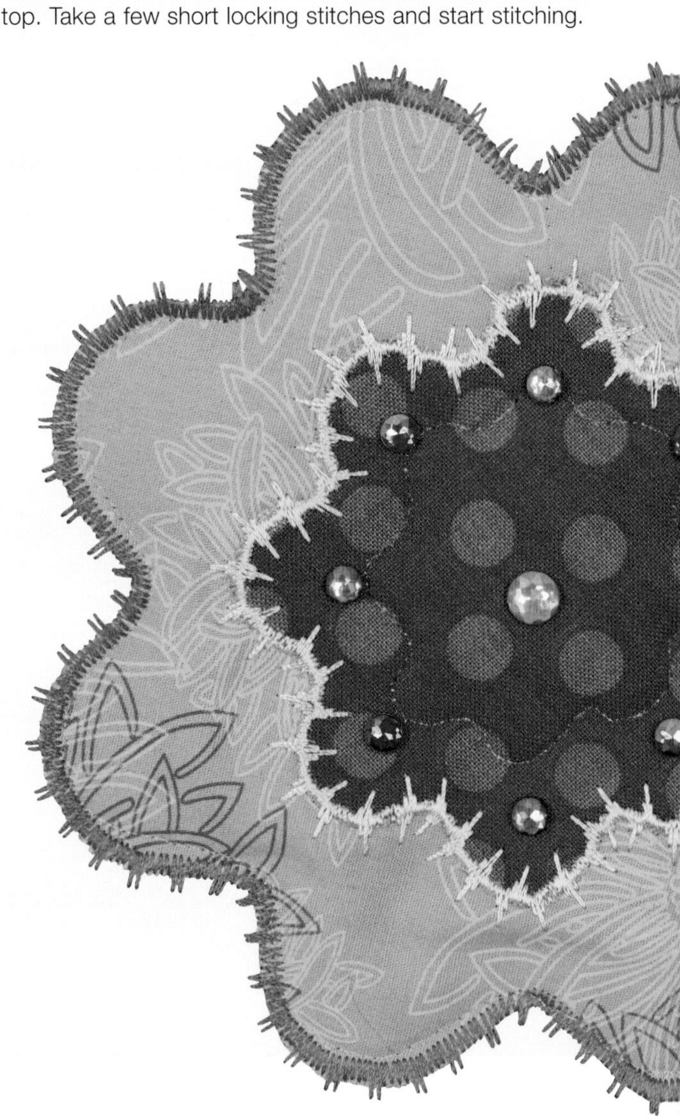

Stabilizing for machine stitching

If using fused appliqué and stitching with a fine zigzag or narrow satin zigzag stitch, I generally do not use stabilizer. In this situation there are two layers of fabric and the fusing glue acts as a stabilizer.

It is often necessary to stabilize appliqué shapes to prevent puckering when:

- using stitches that make wide zigzags or swings of the needle
- stitching a bias edge, such as circles
- doing concentrated stitching in one area
- stitching in an area with one thickness of fabric

Make a test sample using the stitching style and fabrics you will be working with to see if you need additional stabilizer.

A piece of sheet stabilizer, see page 108, is placed under the appliqué and should be removed after stitching. The stitch sample in this photo shows puckering on the left line of satin zigzag stitching where there was no stabilizer. Carefully tear or cut away stabilizer after stitching.

Setting up for machine stitching and embellishing appliqué

You will use the same basic setup for all machine stitching applique. Many of the samples in this section are stitched with a contrasting thread to illustrate the stitches more clearly.

1. Choose a needle that will work best for your fabric and thread combination. Use a smaller needle for finer fabrics, as well as monofilament and finer threads. A larger needle should be used for decorative threads and heavier fabrics. A specialty needle may be needed for some decorative threads. For most appliqué, I use a size 70 or 80 topstitch or sharp needle.
2. Use an open-toe, embroidery, or appliqué presser foot to clearly see the edges, curves, and points of the appliqué shapes as you stitch. All of these presser feet have a wide groove on the underside to accommodate the buildup of thread.
3. Use a bobbin thread that matches the weight of the top thread for easiest tension control. If changing the top thread color frequently or using a heavy, decorative stitch such as satin zigzag, it may be helpful to use a neutral color, very thin polyester bobbin-weight thread. This will not build up on the underside like a heavier thread. If you use a bobbin thread that is not the same weight as the top thread you may need to adjust the upper thread tension. The bobbin thread should not show through on the top of the appliqué. It is preferable if a small amount of top thread can be seen on the wrong side. This helps to create sharp zigs on the top.
4. Make a test sample using the needle, thread, and fabric combination you will be working with for each project. Test various stitches, widths, and lengths. After choosing the stitch combination you want to use, be sure to label the test sample with it. Although I suggest width and length settings under each stitch type, these will differ from machine to machine.

Fine Zigzag Stitch

Two types of zigzag stitches are used for machine appliqué. Fine zigzag stitches are narrow and slightly spaced apart. Satin zigzag stitches, which can be narrow, wide, or decorative, are spaced very close together. Both types of stitches can be used for fused appliqué, as well as turned edge appliqué.

Fine zigzag stitching is recommended for fusible-web-backed appliqué because the fused adhesive is already holding the fabric to the background. This stitching will hold the appliqué pieces in place for gentle washing and drying. When using a thread that matches the fabric this fine zigzag will almost disappear.

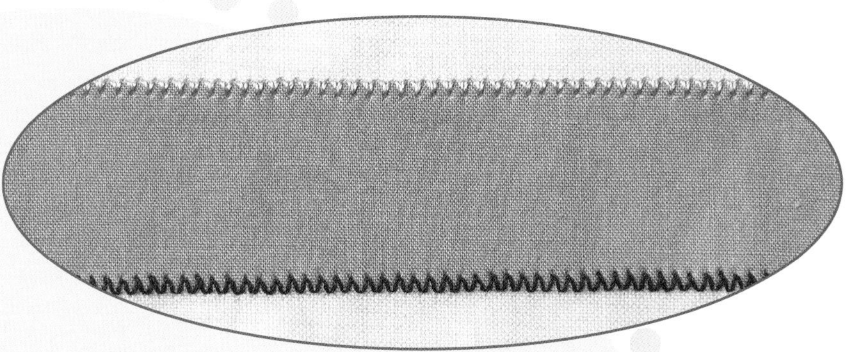

Stitching Instructions

- The fine zigzag stitch should be approximately 1.8 mm to 2 mm wide and .7mm long. It should secure just the edge of the appliqué. I usually use 40-weight rayon or polyester or 60-weight cotton embroidery thread in a color that matches the appliqué fabric.
- Position the presser foot so the right swing of the stitch will be next to the edge of the appliqué. The left swing of the needle will then come onto the appliqué. Begin stitching at the junction of two pieces or along a continuous edge.

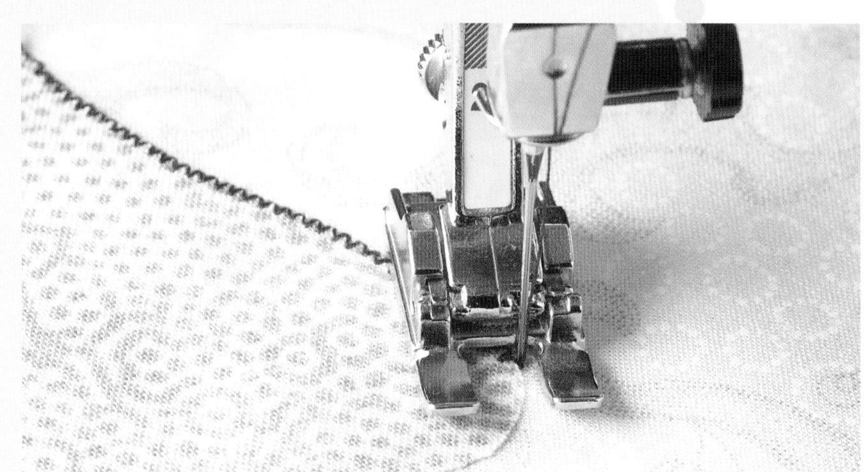

tip

Avoiding frayed edges

If the right swing of the fine or satin zigzag stitch is on the appliqué it may cause fraying, especially on a loosely woven fabric. If the stitches are too far to the right the appliqué may tear out or the background may pucker.

Stitching Corners

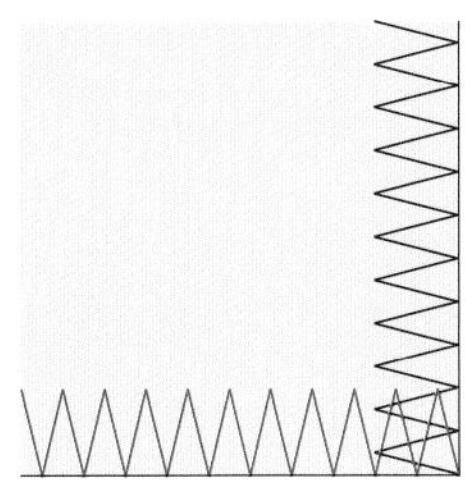

Outside Corners

To stitch an outside corner, stitch to the end of the appliqué and stop with the needle down on the right edge. Raise the presser foot, pivot the fabric, lining up with the next side, lower the presser foot, and continue stitching.

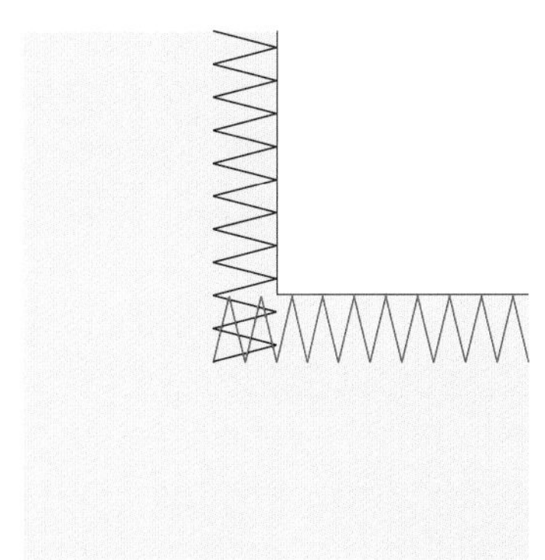

Inside Corners

An inside corner is stitched by stitching past the corner one or two stitches. Stop with needle down on the left side. Raise the presser foot and pivot the fabric, lining up with the next edge. Lower the presser foot and continue stitching. If the corner is less than 90°, move the fabric slightly so the first right stitch is within the previous stitches.

Stitching Curves

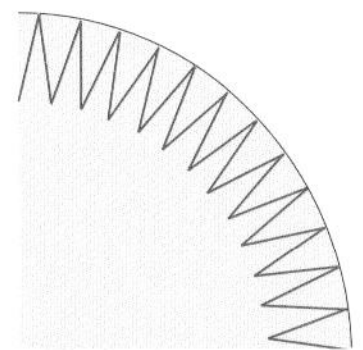

Outside Curves

When stitching outside curves, occasionally pivot the appliqué. Stop with the needle down on the right swing, raise the presser foot and pivot the appliqué slightly, lower the presser foot, and continue stitching. The tightness of the curve will dictate how often you need to pivot. If you do not pivot with the needle down on the right swing, there will be gaps in the stitches.

Inside Curves

When stitching inside curves, occasionally pivot the appliqué. Stop with the needle down on the left swing, raise the presser foot and pivot the appliqué slightly, lower the presser foot, and continue stitching. The tightness of the curve will dictate how often you need to pivot. If you do not pivot with the needle down on the left swing, there will be gaps in the stitches on the appliqué.

Stitching Points

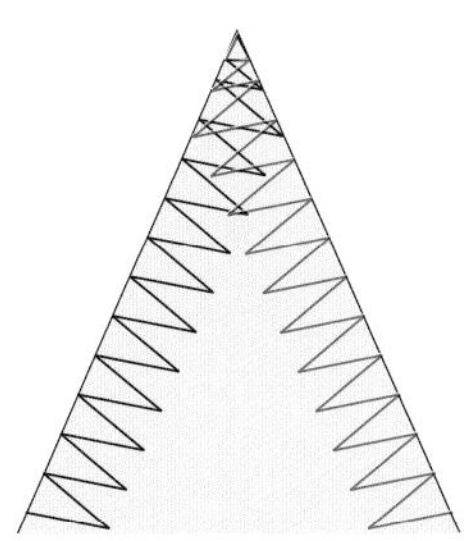

Tapered Points

For a tapered point, stitch to the end of the appliqué corner, decreasing the stitch width the last few stitches and stopping with the needle down on the right edge. Raise the presser foot and pivot the fabric, lining up with the next side. Lower the presser foot, take one stitch, then gradually increase the stitch width until the stitching is at the original setting. This will only be a few stitches. Continue stitching.

Satin Zigzag Stitch

Satin zigzag stitching is recommended for fusible-web-backed appliqué. The fused adhesive holds the appliqué fabric to the background, making it easy to stitch around. This stitching will hold the appliqué pieces in place for regular washing and drying. It makes a solid line of stitching that can be stitched in a variety of widths. The satin zigzag stitch is more decorative than the fine zigzag stitch because it makes a more solid line and when stitched in a contrasting value or color will stand out.

Stitching Instructions

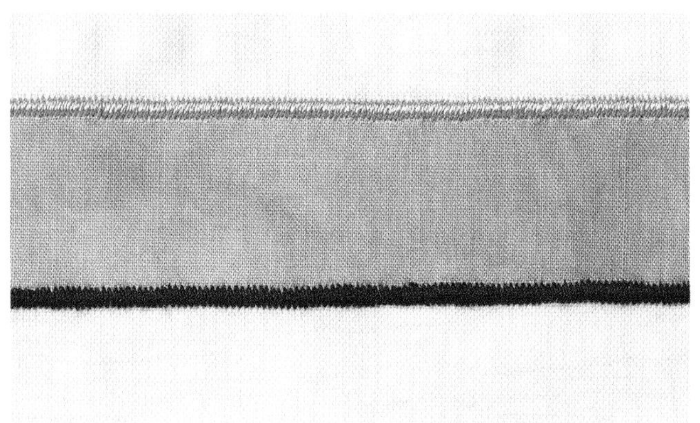

- The satin zigzag stitch should be 2mm to 3.5mm-wide and on a satin setting. It should secure just the edge of the appliqué. I usually use 40-weight rayon or polyester or 60-weight cotton embroidery thread in a color that matches or contrasts with the appliqué fabric.

- Position the presser foot so the right swing of the stitch will be next to the edge of the appliqué. The left swing of the needle will then come onto the appliqué. Begin stitching at the junction of two pieces or along a continuous edge.

Stitching Corners

Corners and curves are stitched in much the same way as fine zigzag stitching, as shown on page 117. Stitch a mitered corner if your satin stitch is 3mm wide or wider.

Mitered Outside Corners

For a mitered outside corner, move the needle position to the far right. Stitch to the end of the appliqué corner; stop with the needle down on the right edge. Raise the presser foot, pivot the fabric, lining up with the next side. Reduce the stitch width to almost zero. Lower the presser foot; stitching slowly, gradually increase stitch width to original setting until the stitching meets the previously stitched line. This will only be a few stitches. Continue stitching.

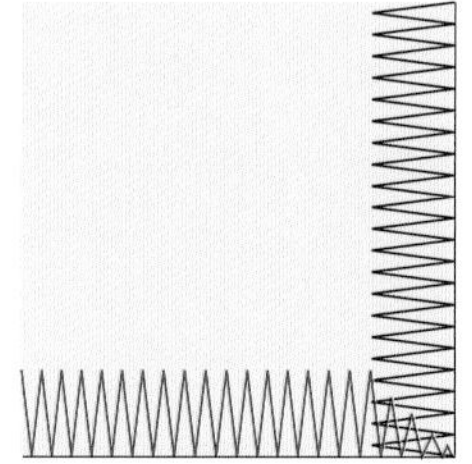

tip

Programmed satin stitches

Your machine may have other programmed satin stitches that work well on the edge of an appliqué as embellishment. Make a test sample, marking the pattern number and any changes made in the width or length.

Blanket Stitch

The blanket, or buttonhole, stitch can be used with fused edge or turned edge appliqué. The blanket stitch gives a crisp look to the edges of appliqué and is used to mimic broderie perse and other nostalgic appliqué such as Sunbonnet Sue.

Stitching Instructions

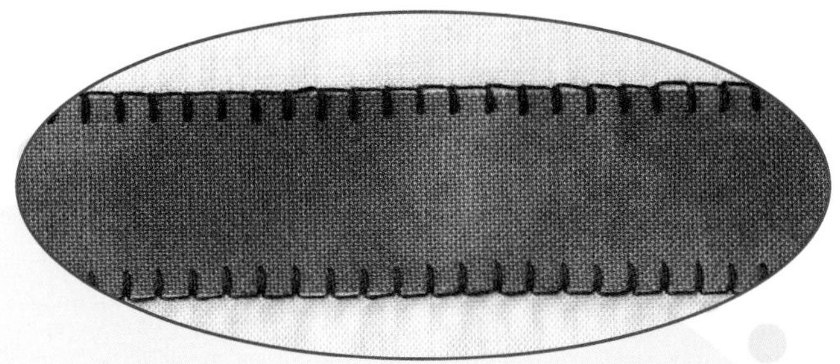

- Threads used most often for the blanket stitch are 50- or heavier weight black or dark colored cotton thread.
- The blanket stitch is a programmed stitch on most sewing machines. There may be more than one variation so choose the best one for your project. Make a stitch sample and test various widths, lengths, and threads to achieve the look you want.
- Position the presser foot so the forward stitches of the blanket stitch are along the right edge of the appliqué but not so close that they are hidden by the appliqué edge. The left swing of the needle will then come onto the appliqué. Begin stitching at the junction of two pieces or along a continuous line.
- For an invisible blanket stitch on turned edge appliqué, use monofilament thread and make the stitch narrower than programmed in the machine.

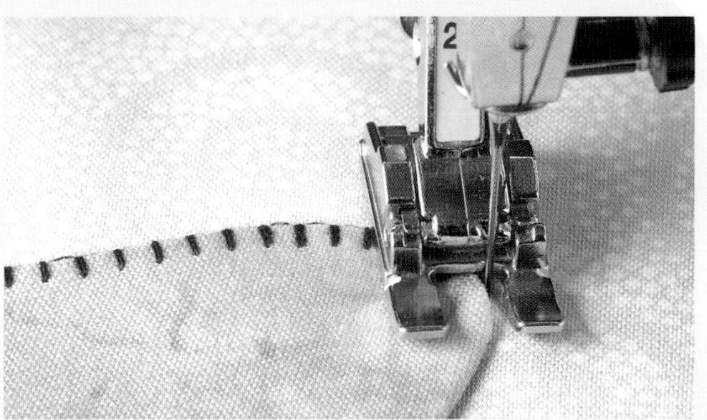

Blind Hem – invisible machine stitch

For invisible machine appliqué use the blind hem or vari-overlock stitch. Blind hem stitching is recommended for turned edge appliqué to give the look and feel of hand appliqué. Some stitchers use a very small blanket stitch with monofilament thread to achieve the hand-stitched appearance.

Stitching Instructions

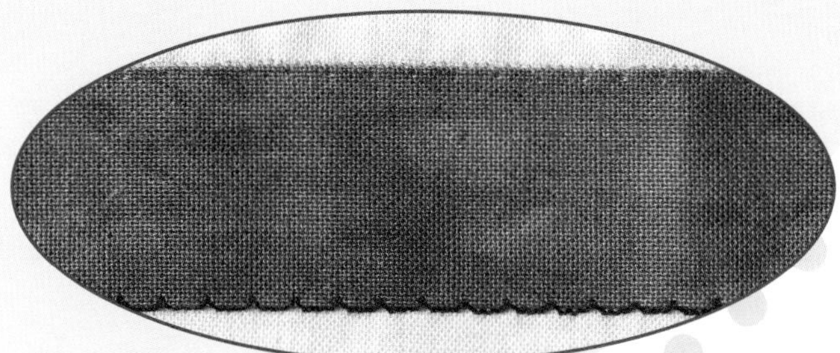

- The top thread should be invisible monofilament nylon or polyester thread. You can also use a 60-weight cotton or silk thread in a color that matches the appliqué fabric exactly. In the bobbin use 60-weight cotton or polyester thread in a color that matches the appliqué background.
- In most instances a .1mm-wide and .1mm-long stitch will work best. There should be approximately 1/8" between bites, two to four forward stitches, and each bite (zig to the left) should catch one or two threads of the appliqué piece. Since machines vary, make a stitch sample and test various widths and lengths to achieve an invisible hand appliqué look.
- Position the presser foot so the forward stitches are along the edge of the appliqué and the left swing of the needle will then come on to the appliqué. Begin stitching at the junction of two pieces or anywhere on a continuous line.

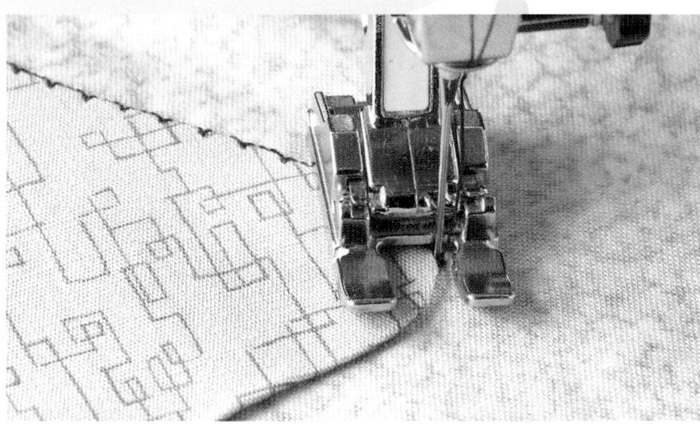

embellishing

Embellishing can add special spark and texture to appliqué. Decorative stitching can be used in place of fine or satin zigzag edge stitching and can be added to any of the quilt projects in this book. Beading and other decorative embellishing may be added to wallhangings or projects for older children.

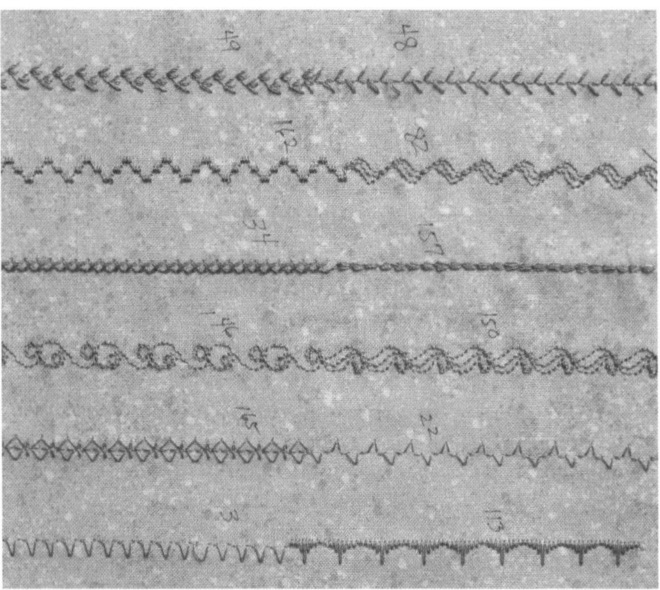

- Make a stitch sample and test various width and length combinations. Usually you will use the preset programmed length and width, but mark the test sample with the stitch number and any length or width changes.

Programmed Stitches

One of the easiest ways to embellish machine appliqué is with the programmed stitches found on your sewing machine. These stitches can add life-like texture to your appliqué. Use contrasting or decorative thread that will show off the stitching.

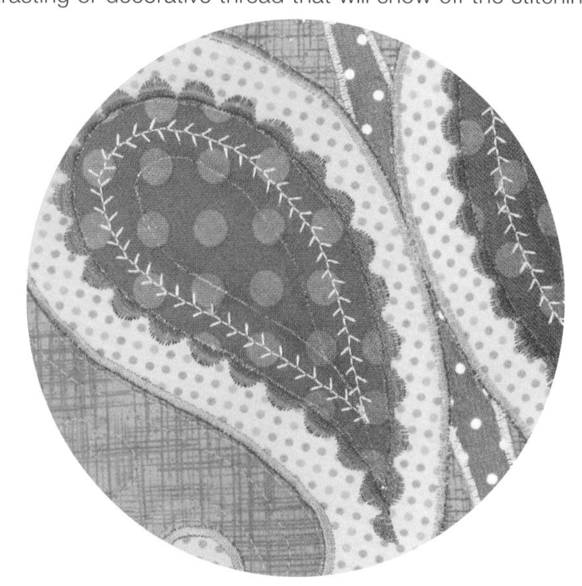

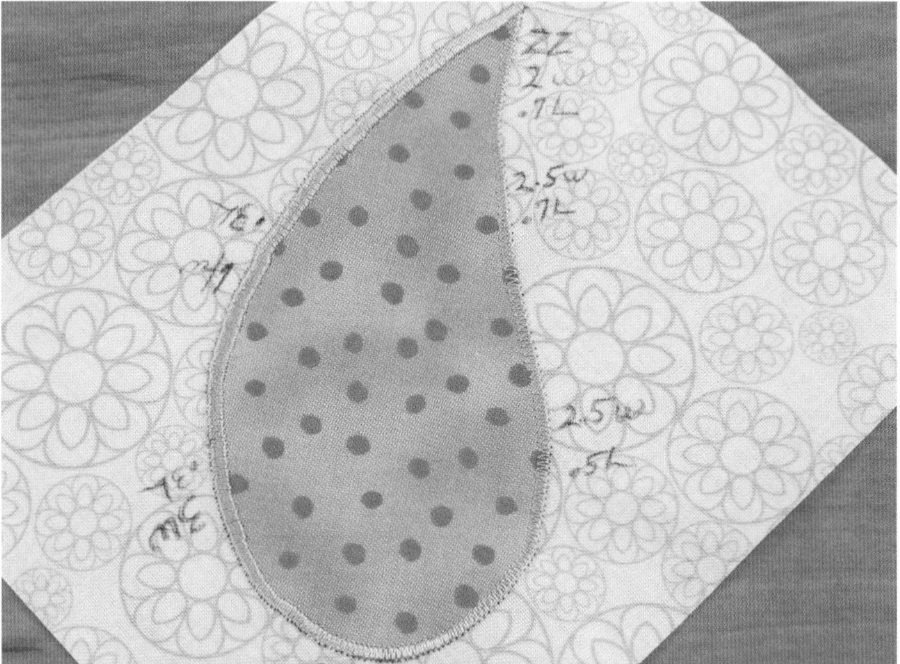

- Make a sample using your appliqué fabrics and threads. Test various stitch widths to achieve the look you want.

Satin Zigzag Stitch

The satin zigzag stitch is great for adding a contrasting line to any appliqué. It can help differentiate between appliqué pieces or define a line. Choose a thread color that enhances the appliqué. For a delicate look, use rayon or shiny polyester. For a heavier more definitive edge, use 50-weight or heavier cotton thread.

Stitching Mouths and Lines

Two programmed stitches, the triple straight stitch and satin zigzag stitch, can be used to create lines for mouths such as the Paisley Princess on page 40 or a bug's antennae. Each stitch gives a different look. Make a sample of each stitch for reference.

The sample above shows a line of triple stitch using 50-weight cotton thread, a line of triple stitch using 40-weight rayon and a line of satin zigzag stitch using 40-weight rayon.

Triple Straight Stitch

Most sewing machines have a triple straight stitch. This stitch moves forward, back and then forward again before starting the next stitch. This sequence creates a heavier line. The triple stitch can be tricky to use when going around curves. You must make all directional changes, even very small ones, by pivoting at the beginning of the sequence. Stabilize if necessary.

Satin Zigzag Stitch

For a wider line use a satin zigzag stitch. Make samples of different widths to determine what will work best for your project. You can increase or decrease the width of the line as you stitch. Stabilize wider stitching if necessary.

Stitching the line

1. Using the template from your project, use a permanent marker or pencil to trace or draw the line you want to stitch on tissue paper or tear away stabilizer. Place in position on the appliqué. Straight stitch on the line. Tear away the paper.

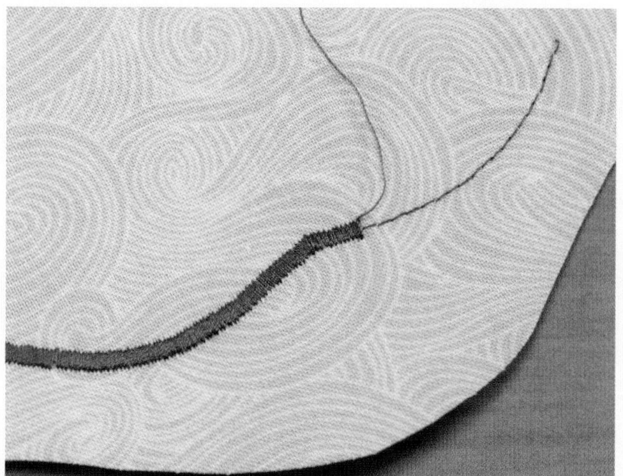

2. Insert stabilizer under the area and stitch over the straight stitch with desired width satin zigzag.

Note: You may also use a pencil, removable marker, or chalk to mark the line you wish to stitch directly on the appliqué. Stitch on the line, using stabilizer on the back.

Other Embellishments

Many embellishments are easiest to add after a project has been layered and quilted. A quilt with beads and crystals needs to be hand washed.

Beading

Putting beads, buttons, sequins and other decorations on your finished project adds extra dimension and glitz to your quilt. **Do not use beads or other surface embellishment on quilts or items for younger children, as these could pose a choking hazard.**

An assortment of beads

Types of beads

Beads come in glass, plastic, and metal with various finishes from matte to shiny. Some beads are available in shapes such as hearts, teardrops, flowers, and leaves or have multifaceted sides. Due to the popularity of beading there are many new shapes and finishes in beads.

Two very common bead types are seed beads and bugle beads. Seed beads have a round squat shape and come in several sizes. The most common seed bead sizes are 14, 11, and 8, with the larger number representing the smaller bead. Bugle beads are long and narrow. They come in sizes 1 to 5 and are sometimes measured in millimeters (5 mm). Bugle beads have very sharp ends because they have been cut.

Threads for beading

Threads designed specifically for beading come waxed and unwaxed and are often made of nylon. It is not required to have waxed thread for attaching beads to a quilt but it can prevent some tangles. Regular 50- or 40-weight cotton thread can also be used. Use a neutral gray, taupe, or buckskin color or a color to match the beads or the quilt fabric.

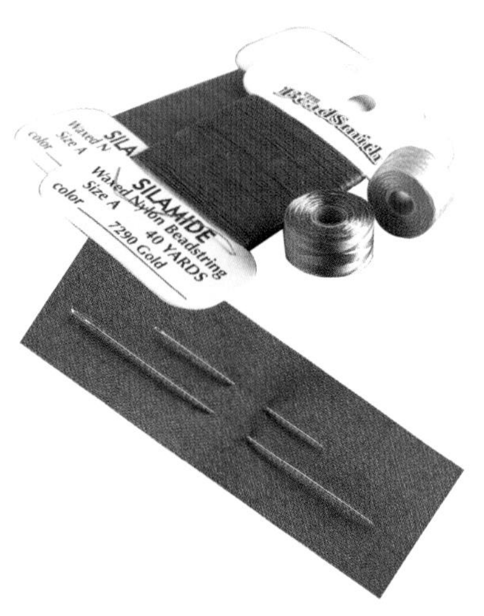

Needles for beading

Betweens or Sharps #10 or #12 will go through the seed and bugle beads in the sizes mentioned and are easy to use for quilt beading. Beading needles, which are about 2" long and very fine, may bend when working through layered or quilted appliqué.

Basic Beading Technique

Although you can add beads to appliqué before it is layered, thus hiding any stitching, it may be difficult to machine quilt around the beads. The following technique for adding beads is similar to hand quilting.

Work with a knotted length of thread about 18" long. Insert the needle from the front of the appliqué. Bring the needle to the surface where you want to add the first bead and pull the knot into the layers just as you do when hand quilting.

Place a bead on the needle. At the width of the bead or beads, insert needle into the layers and move to the next position.

Secure the beads as you go by making a small backstitch or knot on the back of the project every three or four beads or groups of beads. By doing this, you will only lose a few beads if thread breaks.

End the beading by making a knot and pulling it into the layers. Clip the thread.

Two sizes of beads are used to secure a flower-shaped sequin to the edge of this appliqué.

tip

Threading beads to needle

Place beads in a lid or shallow bowl. To thread a bead on your needle, insert the needle in the hole of the bead and push slightly against the side of the hole. The bead will pop onto the needle.

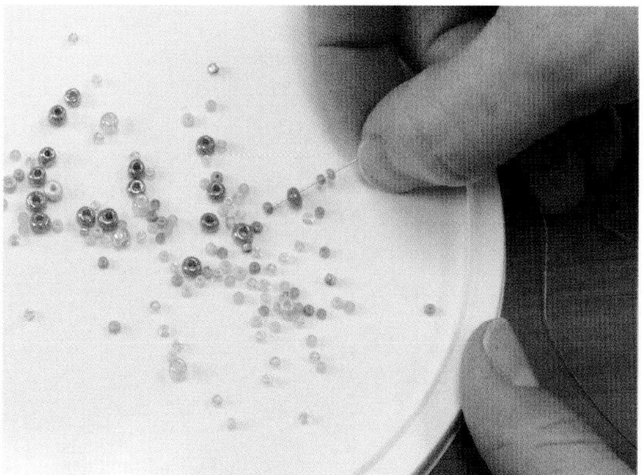

Beading Examples

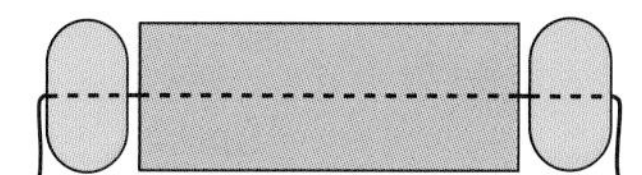

For bugle beads that have sharp cut ends, add a seed bead at both ends.

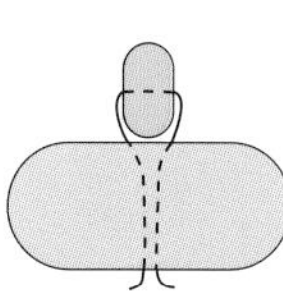

For larger beads or sequins that you want to lie flat, add a seed bead on top and pass the thread back through the larger bead or sequin.

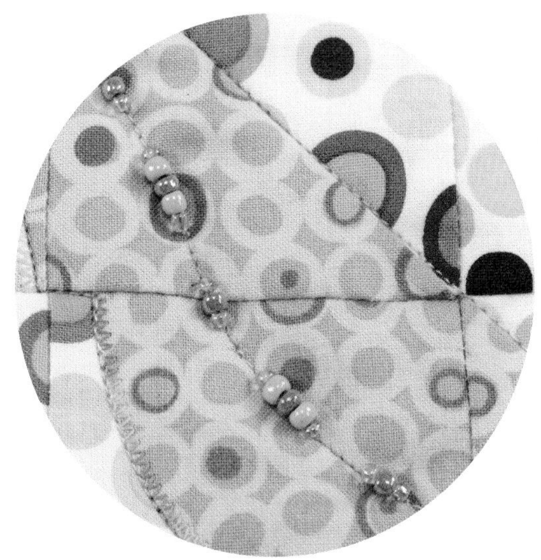

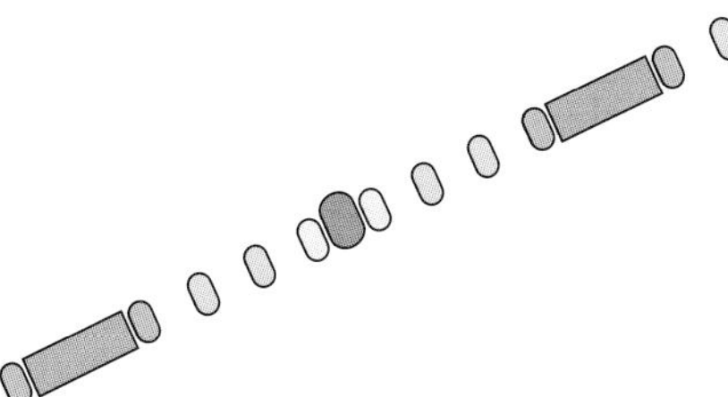

For decorative lines of beads, repeat the same grouping of beads at regular intervals, or intersperse sets of beads with single beads.

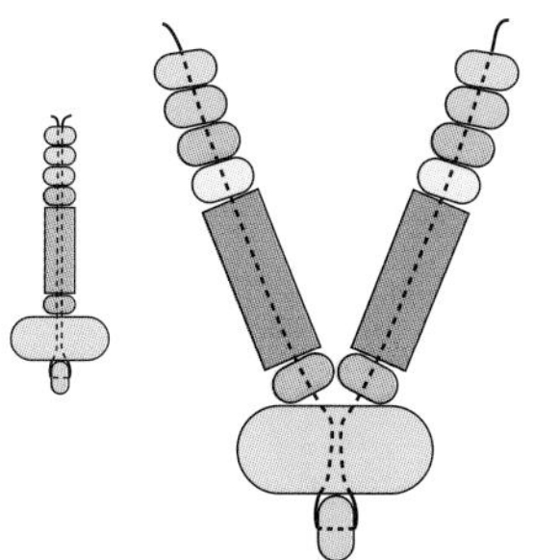

For bead dangles, thread several beads onto the thread. For the center, add a larger bead or charm. Bring the thread up to the starting point or, after going back through a few beads veer off with another string of beads.

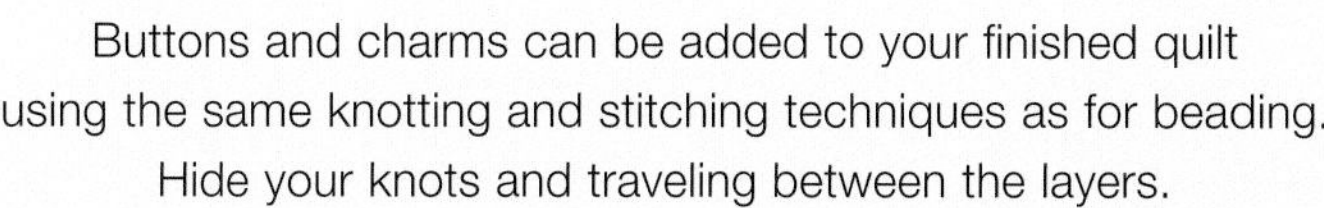

Buttons and charms can be added to your finished quilt using the same knotting and stitching techniques as for beading. Hide your knots and traveling between the layers.

Couching Ribbons and Yarns

Decorative ribbons and yarns can be couched on quilts in place of appliqué or decorative stitching. For machine couching, use zigzag, programmed, or free-motion stitching to secure ribbons or yarns to the quilt. I usually do this at the appliqué and stitching stage.

- Couch a dark textured yarn to simulate the tract on the Construction Zone backhoe and bulldozer in place of the decorative triangle satin stitch used.
- For the wand stick on Bedazzled Princess on page 44, I used a pink satin ribbon stitched down with a programmed feather stitch.

Crystals

You can apply real Swarovski crystals, rhinestones, or inexpensive glass or plastic jewels to bedazzle a wallhanging. I usually add these after quilting and binding a project.

- Some Swarovski crystals and rhinestones, pearls and metal studs come with a pre-glued backing which must be applied to the fabric with a special heat applicator. These embellishments are also available with no glue backing and can be applied with fabric glue.
- You can find inexpensive press-on crystals at craft stores. Once applied to fabric they will stay unless brushed or pried off. Buy extra as they make great collage decorations and ear studs for little girls.

Heat-Bondable Fibers

Angelina and Crystalina fibers are made of thinly cut strips of polyester film and are washable. The fibers come in many colors and values. When heated these fibers bond to themselves forming a fabric that is often iridescent. I used Crystalina to make a halo behind the Bedazzled Princess star on page 44.

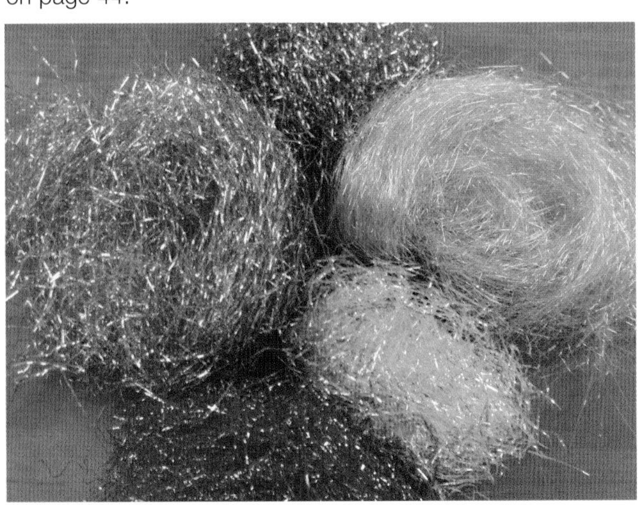

Unironed Ironed

- Take a small amount of the fiber and place between pieces of parchment paper or a non-stick pressing sheet to protect your iron.
- Set the iron on a silk setting and press the fibers for two or three seconds. The longer you press the smoother it gets. The color will also change with more heat.

Transferring Photos to Fabric

To transfer a photograph to fabric, use one of the methods below.

Copy Machine

Iron-on transfer paper is a pretreated sheet that photographs or other images can be copied on and then ironed onto fabric to transfer the image. Copy the image in reverse. This is especially important if there are any words or objects on the image that would obviously appear as backward. Follow manufacturer's instructions to determine the heat setting for the type of fabric you are using. For best transfer results use high count white muslin and a dry iron.

Computer and Printer

- Pretreated fabric sheets, such as Printed Treasures™ and EQ Printables, are designed to accept ink and are paper-backed and ready for an inkjet printer. Epson® inkjet inks are archival and are therefore preferred over HP inks. Follow manufacturer's instructions for heat setting.
- To treat your own fabric, use a product such as Bubble Jet Set on very high count pima cotton (200) if available. Iron the fabric to the shiny side of freezer paper then cut into 8½" x 11" sheets.
- When using a printer you must have your photograph and/or label information loaded into the computer. If printing only photographs, they can be printed directly from a photo utility program. To combine photos and text you will need to have a program designed to let you use both, such as a word processing program.

These photos are printed on a pretreated fabric sheet. The photo on the left is brighter and the colors are more saturated than the photo on the right. It also has higher contrast.

- To make adjustments in your photographs before printing to fabric, you need a photo editing program. This program has tools that allow you to resize and crop your photos. It also gives you the ability to adjust the photo's brightness, contrast, and color saturation. Fabric is a flat, matte surface and making the colors brighter and more saturated and increasing the contrast may make a better printed photograph. Make a test sample with a photograph you might want to print to fabric. Make a few changes at a time, save the changes and then print several samples with notes on a sheet of prepared fabric and on your usual printer paper. You can compare these sheets and refer to them when working with other photographs.

finishing kids quilts

Be sure to label your quilt so future generations can treasure the love and care put into your project.

Quilting Appliqué

Layer and pin the backing, batting, and quilt top in the usual manner. When I quilt my projects, I begin by quilting in the ditch around any borders and major blocks. For this type of stitching I use a walking foot to secure the quilt layers. I change to a darning or free-motion foot and monofilament thread or thread to match the background fabric when I quilt around the appliqué motifs. I add some quilting in the motif to add texture and emphasize the character, then quilt the background to make the appliqué motif stand out.

Labeling

It is very important to add a label to any quilt with the name of the maker and the date. Labels on quilts for kids can be personalized to let the recipient know and remember who made the quilt and if it was made for a special occasion. I try to put the label on the quilt before quilting or at least before binding so the label becomes a permanent part of the quilt.

Label information can include:
Name of maker and address
Date quilt was made
Quilt pattern name
Who the quilt was made for
Special occasion
(i.e., birthday, Christmas)

- You can make a machine or hand stitched label on light colored fabric. Many of today's sewing machines include alphabet letters as one of their programmed stitches.
- You can also make your own hand-printed label by cutting a piece of freezer paper the size of your label. Use a ruler to mark the dull side with evenly spaced dark lines. Iron a piece of light colored fabric to the shiny side of the freezer paper. The lines should show through to provide guidelines for hand printing your label with a fine-tip permanent marking pen.
- You can purchase decorative labels and fill in the important information with permanent marking pen. Follow manufacturer's directions for setting the ink.
- Using your computer, type the label information and print onto purchased prepared inkjet printable fabric sheets. Refer to Transferring Photos to Fabric on page 125 and add a photo of yourself, the recipient, or a favorite memory along with the other information on the computer.

Binding

Bind your quilt using your favorite method. For a stronger binding, I pin the binding over to the back and top-stitch in the ditch on the quilt front.

Block Play Grids

Copy the Block Play Grids below at 300% or create your own $7\frac{1}{2}$" grids.

Block Play 9-Patch

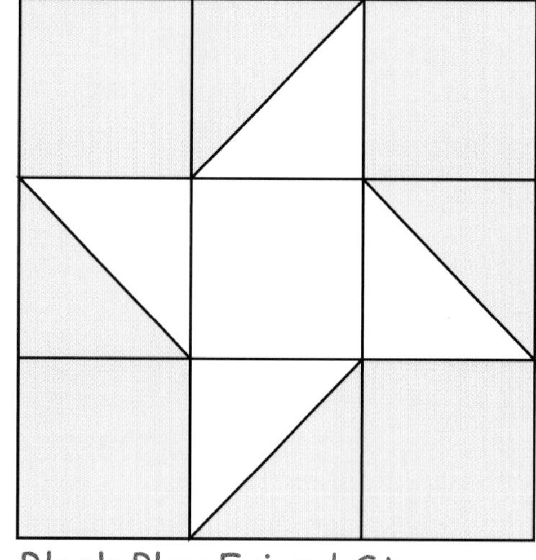

Block Play Friend Star

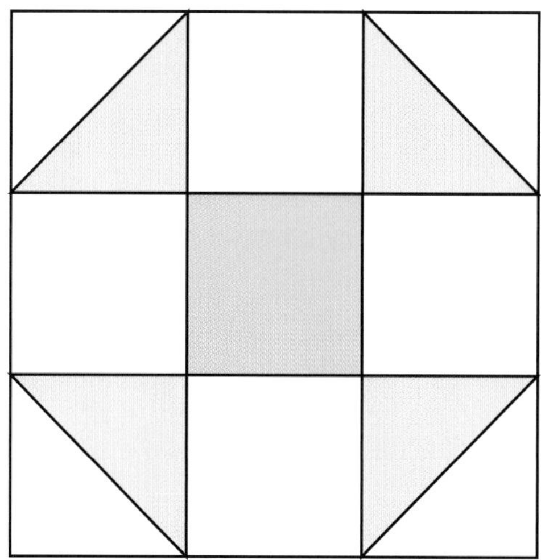

Block Play Shoofly

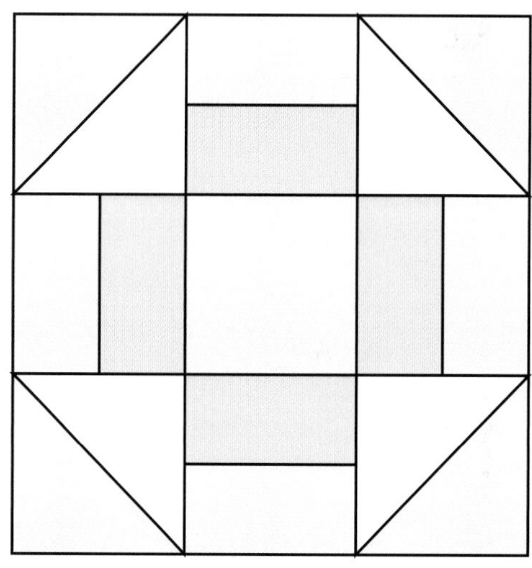

Block Play Churn Dash

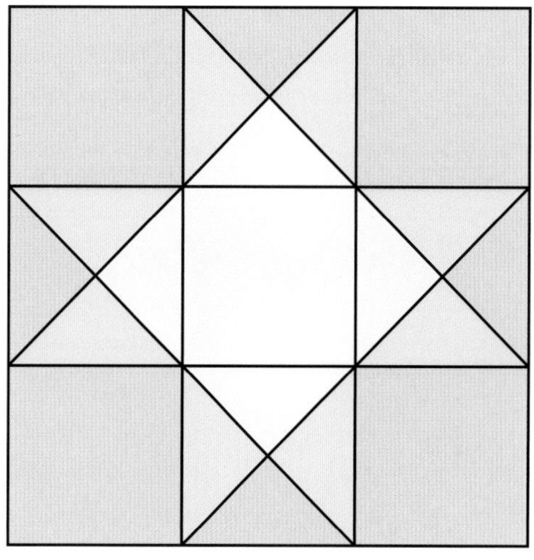

Block Play Ohio Star

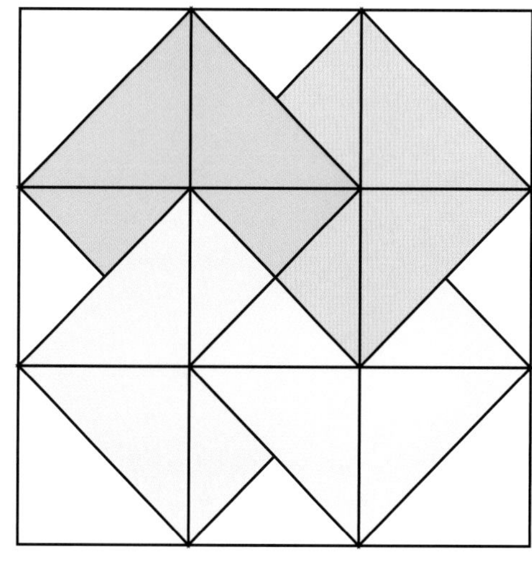

Block Play Card Trick

Block Play Grids

Copy the Block Play Grids below at 300%, create your own 7½" grids, or download at www.landauerpub.com.

Block Play 9-Patch

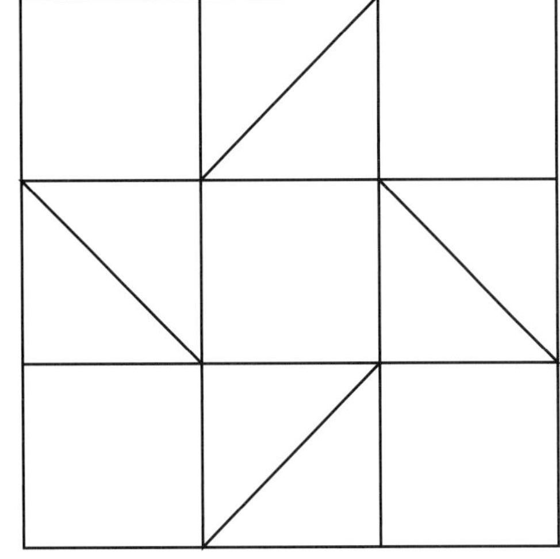

Block Play Friend Star

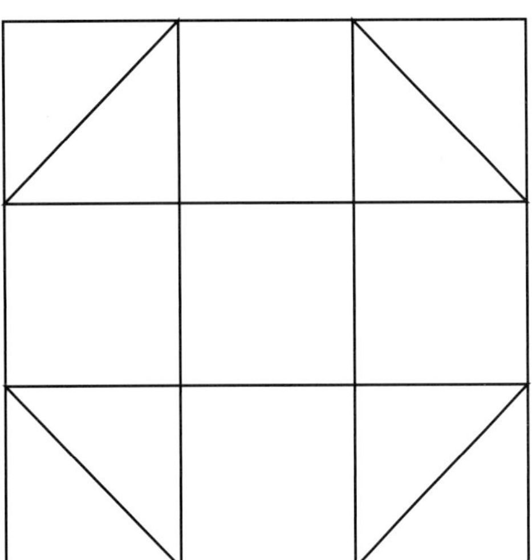

Block Play Shoofly

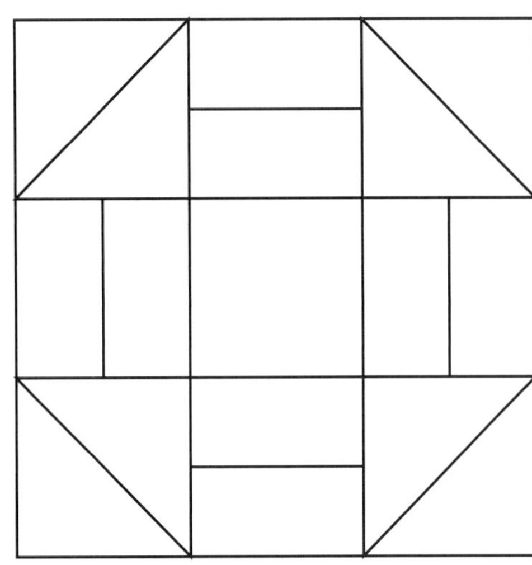

Block Play Churn Dash

Block Play Ohio Star

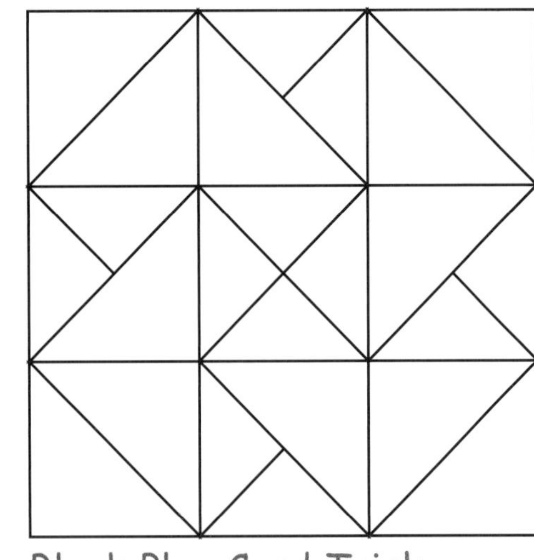

Block Play Card Trick